When the Minister
Is a *Woman*

Dear Annie,
    I have been blessed with
knowing you and having you
as a dear friend. I have learned
so much from you about faith
in God and strength that comes
from Him. You are my inspiration.
God Bless you with grace & peace.
                              Love
                              your
                              Friend,
                              Barbara J.
                              Rhodes

When the Minister Is a Woman

Debra E. Harmon
Barbara J. Rhodes

CHALICE
PRESS

ST. LOUIS, MISSOURI

Cover image: FotoSearch
Cover and interior design: Elizabeth Wright

Visit Chalice Press on the World Wide Web at
www.chalicepress.com

10 9 8 7 6 5 4 3 2 1   08 09 10 11 12

Library of Congress Cataloging-in-Publication Data

Harmon, Debra E.

When the minister is a woman / Debra E. Harmon and Barbara J. Rhodes.

p. cm.

ISBN 978-0-8272-4256-2

1. Women clergy. I. Rhodes, Barbara J. II. Title.

BV676.H37 2008

253'.2082—dc22   2008012066

Printed in United States of America

*To my husband and children, friends, colleagues,
and churches I have served for giving me affirmation
and encouragement in my ministry.*

> *Thank you for everything,*
> *Barbara*

*To my husband, Bob, my colleague in ministry,
who makes me glad to be a woman.*

> *DEH*

Contents

Introduction

Most women in ministry, if not all, have a fascinating story about their journey. If you ask, it doesn't take long before you hear great stories of being called, of deep faith and commitment, of sacrifice and discovery. Some have struggled against incredible odds; some have overcome challenges from within and without; some continue to meet obstacles to their ministry with grace and good will. Every clergywoman has a story, and in sharing those stories we are strengthened and encouraged.

In July of 2005, at the General Assembly of the Christian Church (Disciples of Christ) in Portland, Oregon, I (Debra Harmon) asked Trent Butler, then Editorial Director of the Chalice Press, about a book idea I had been working on. While encouraging, he told me what he was really looking for was a book for and about women in ministry, about a woman's experience in ministry, about the unique joys and the challenges that women face.

Well, I know something about that. I was ordained in the Christian Church (Disciples of Christ) in June of 1994, a month after completing my Master of Divinity degree at Christian Theological Seminary in Indianapolis. While a seminary student, I served as a part-time associate minister of youth at a United Methodist Church for almost two years. My first fulltime ministry position was as an associate minister of youth and family ministries at a church in central Indiana, where I spent seven years. I completed a year of clinical pastoral education in Indianapolis, and am now pastor of a small church in Virginia. I have officiated at about twenty-five weddings and at least as many funerals in my first ten years of ministry. As I said, I know something about a woman's experience in ministry.

I think we as women bring some unique gifts and talents to the ministry. In the summer of 2006 I attended the "Mix in '06," a gathering of women of the Christian Church (Disciples of Christ) and the United Church of Christ. The energy among the three thousand women was marvelous. Church secretaries and women's group presidents mingled with and encouraged ordained and licensed clergywomen. Women led worship and workshops, organized mission efforts and ministry exhibits, and illustrated what an amazing force women are in the church. This was just one event, just a sampling of all the ministry women do in the church.

With women now being ordained and licensed in most mainline Protestant denominations, particularly in the past few decades, they bring a new voice, a new complexion to the church. Church has a more balanced feel, a broader perspective, a fuller sound. We bring women and women's issues to the forefront, whereas before they were swept quietly to the side, or assigned to the women's group of the church. We bring women's wisdom and experience, and ways of doing things, which benefit the body of Christ as a whole.

The presence of women in the pulpit, wearing the robes and stoles of clergy, officiating at sacred ceremonies such as baptism, marriage, communion, and funerals, makes sacred the feminine energy they bring to the task. Having women visible as clergy makes sacred the other half of humanity, the half that has long been denied a presence in such sacred ways. Women's voices have called us to conceive of God in different ways as well—as a loving mother, as a passionate spouse, as a hen protecting her chicks.

Women have asked questions and challenged the status quo. Not content with, "We've always done it this way," we think of new ways of doing the work of the church, of pastoring and administering and leading. We imagine new vistas, dream new dreams, see visions of what can be, and then work to bring them about.

But to write a book about it? Aren't there enough books about women in ministry? There are books such as *A Woman in the Pulpit*, by Carol M. Noren; and *And Blessed Is She*, edited by David Albert Farmer and Edwina Hunter, about women's sermons and preaching styles. There have been studies done, such as *The Stained Glass Ceiling: Churches and Their Women Pastors,* by Sally B. Purvis; and the comprehensive work done in *Clergy Women: An Uphill Calling,* by Barbara Brown Zikmund, Adair Lummis, and Patricia Chang. They completed almost five thousand surveys among clergy women in sixteen mainline Protestant denominations and found that while the experience of ministry is generally improving, most women are still at mid-level and in parachurch positions.

The work of Zikmund, Lummis, and Chang, though, however enlightening, was largely statistical. What we want to do in this book is look at women's *experience* of ministry: practical concerns particular to women in ministry, the joys and celebrations of women in ministry, some of the unique obstacles and challenges of women in ministry, the gifts and talents women bring to their ministry. What are some of the special, sacred moments that we as women enjoy? What are some of the more amusing stories? (If you are in ministry more than five minutes, you are bound to have some of those.) What are some practical considerations that women need to be aware of, and prepare themselves for, such as negotiating a fair contract? Where do we find images, particularly in the Judeo-Christian tradition, that feed our feminine spirits, as well as lift up and celebrate women as sacred creatures, worthy to be called to ministry? And how do we balance being clergywomen with all the other demands on us, from our families, our friends, and our own bodies and spirits?

Who is this book for? Who is our intended audience? This book is intended first of all for women who are considering a call to ministry, women who are in seminary pursuing that call, or women who are at the beginning of their professional ministry. We have written with you in mind. The stories and anecdotes contained here are from women who have been at it for a while. We will look at some of the specific concerns of women clergy, such as how to balance their many roles of daughter, sister, wife, mother, grandmother, and friend with their calling as a minister. We want you to benefit from our experience, to give you a "heads up" on aspects of ministry you might not expect, maybe to forewarn you where some landmines are, but most of all to let you know the water's fine—plunge on in!

This book will hopefully show how women's unique gifts and traits help them to be more effective in their ministry. Women are trained from the cradle to be compassionate and sensitive to the needs of others. We are taught to be relational and work within a community. These are highly useful traits when working in churches, and the growing number of women in ministry shows that they bring different and equally effective ways of doing the work of the church. For example, meetings tend to be oriented toward cooperation and consensus rather than divided by competition for control. Leadership tends to be more collegial than corporate. All of this lends itself to living and working together in community.

Now, while intended first for women in ministry or women considering ministry, this book will hopefully benefit others as well. Our brothers in the ministry who read this book may gain a new sense of how our experience of ministry differs from theirs, and perhaps a greater appreciation for some of the unique struggles we face as women in ministry. Also, we hope our brother clergy will see that we share with them a sense of call and purpose, and a deep devotion to the work of the Lord.

Some of our greatest camaraderie and support comes from time with our brothers in the ministry, from seminary on. Swapping stories about juggling schedules, sermon topics, and dealing with our latest overwrought bride is good for all of us. Since seminary, I have treasured working with my brothers in the ministry, and count some of my dearest friends among them. They help me to see things in a different way and are generally encouraging and supportive. But it would also help our male colleagues to understand the challenges we face, as well as gifts we bring as women to the ministry we do.

We hope that as our brothers in ministry work with us, it will broaden their perspective on how ministry can be done. I have the benefit of having an in-house male colleague in my husband, Bob, who is also an ordained minister. He has observed that women need to learn how to work within the traditionally male system and understand the way men work. Fortunately, he also agrees men need to see that women do ministry in their own way, and need to respect any differences as still legitimate ways of doing ministry. He offered the thought that, as in a marriage, perhaps the best ministry will be done when we find a synthesis of both styles of ministry, when we learn to work together, using the gifts and talents of each. At least we as women need to create ties with our brothers in ministry, to balance and broaden our own ministry style. And we hope the men will learn something from us as well.

Likewise, for the family and friends of a woman in the ministry or considering ministry, this book can give you a window into what she might be thinking, feeling, or experiencing. How will she get that paper in for class tomorrow, the sermon written for Sunday, and still get the kids to soccer tonight? Why is it she wants her daughter (and son!) to have some positive, feminine images of God, as well as the more traditional patriarchal fare? How does she deal with the pressures as well as the joys of the ministry she has been called to do? And why does she want to be a minister anyway?

For congregations who have a woman pastor, or who are considering calling a female pastor (or who think they would never even consider having a woman pastor!), this book might give you a sense of the special gifts and graces a woman brings to that special place of leadership in your congregation. Hopefully, it will encourage you to embrace female pastors as leaders for the church today, and welcome them into your congregation.

One caution for those who read this book: we in no way claim that this a definitive work on women's experience in ministry. While we cite the stories of as many women ministers as we can, we know we are only beginning to scratch the surface. There have been women in the ordained ministry for decades, and they have a rich wealth of experience. Today's women in ministry comprise a broad scope of ethnic, cultural, and socioeconomic experience. We do not mean to speak for all women in ministry. In fact, I have to admit some trepidation in writing this book, knowing so many women in ministry have gone before me and have such a wealth of experience. Who am I to write this book?

Many fine women ministers have broken the hallowed ground of ministry before us, and I know many in ministry now who are much wiser and more insightful than I. However, this book is simply meant to add our voices and promote the conversation by women in ministry and about women in ministry. It is meant to encourage others to think about what it might be like to be a woman in ministry, and hopefully to ask some women ministers they know about their experience. Find some of those wise and wonderful women who have been doing ministry awhile and ask them to share their stories. This book is meant to start those conversations and to make us all think a bit more about women in ministry. Consider this book as a starting point and a conversation partner in your journey.

Finally, read this book with a request in mind. We all know about sitting around a table with our girlfriends, drinking a cup of coffee or tea, and sharing stories from our day and the details of our lives (think *The View, Sex in the City,* or *Friends*). Someone will tell something that happened to her, and someone else will share a similar experience. In such informal, conversational settings some of the best stories are told, and some of the greatest moments of *simpatico* are shared. I invite you to read this book as if it were such a conversation over tea or coffee. Sit back, relax, hear the stories of these friends and sisters, make comments as you choose, and share your own story as you go. It might help if you keep a journal by your side as you read, and take time out to respond and comment, or consider how what you have read is reflected in your own life. In these moments of commonality and shared experience we will find we are on this journey together. That is our greatest hope in writing this book, that we will be supported and strengthened by the community and camaraderie we find in sharing our stories together as women in ministry.

As Robert Fulghum, a brother in ministry and one of my favorite writers, said in *All I Really Need to Know I Learned in Kindergarten*, "Wisdom was not at the top of the graduate school mountain, but there in the sand pile at Sunday School…And it is still true, no matter how old you are, when you go out into the world, it is best to hold hands and stick together."[1] In that spirit, let's hold hands and get going.

---

[1]Robert Fulghum, *All I Really Need to Know I Learned in Kindergarten* (New York: Villard Books, 1988), 6, 8.

1

Where Do I Get Waders with Hips?

Every minister has stories: stories about the frantic bride running around in tears at the wedding rehearsal; about the heating element on the state-of-the-art baptistry going awry and turning the sanctuary into a sauna the day of the baptism; about the groom who almost fainted (thank God for kneeling rails!); about the body of the deceased being sent to the wrong funeral home in town, the one with whom the family had had a long-standing feud, although no one could remember exactly what the feud was about. All of these things have happened (trust me!), and they tend to add the spice and the joy to what we do. All ministers have stories they chuckle about, and they will gladly share if given the chance. Women in ministry have some stories that are unique to being a woman. Ours are stories of challenge and of grace, stories of the sublime and the absurd—moments we have met and endured, and enjoy telling about for years afterward! Let these stories amuse and inspire you, as well as show you some of the amazing women in ministry, and the ways they have handled the more ludicrous moments of their lives.

One of the greatest joys of ministry is baptizing new members into the faith. Whether your tradition practices infant baptism or, like mine, believer's baptism with immersion, it is always a sacred time to share with a person and their family. That being said, it is also fraught with potential for funny stories. When I (Debra) was at my first pastorate, I was baptizing a number of members of my youth group one Sunday. One young man, about sixteen years old, was concerned if I could get him under the water. He was a baseball player, of muscular build, and about the same size I was. I promised I would. The grand moment came. His mother and family, as well as the whole congregation were there to witness the joyful event. He stepped down into the water, and I said the prescribed words, "I baptize you in the name of the Father, and of the Son, and of the Holy Spirit." I pushed him down into the water, held him there for a second, and then he came up laughing. At the moment, I was flattered to think he was overcome with the joy of the Lord. I heard members of the congregation laughing as well, and I just attributed it to their sharing in the joy of the moment.

After the service, though, I was illuminated to the source of his laughter. Apparently, as I pushed him under the water, intent on making sure to get him good and baptized, I knocked him off his feet. While I was watching his head, his feet flew up in the air, so that a number of people in the congregation saw them and started laughing. I'm sure it must have been a sight to see, and he never stopped teasing me about it. This was one of my first lessons in that each of us have faults and foibles, none of us are perfect, and we must accept our gaffs with grace.

Those kinds of stories are the inspiration for this chapter. True, there are more weighty issues, theological and philosophical, that we face as women in ministry. But in the practice of ministry, we all come across funny moments—gaffs on either our part or someone else's—that help to make ministry the joy that it is. Again, none of us are perfect, and at times it seems God is intent on reminding us of that. The harder we try to be perfect, the harder the fall when we land flat on our faces. As women who have pushed ourselves to achieve what relatively few women have—seminary education, ordination, a ministry—we might be hardest on ourselves. We need to learn to extend to ourselves the grace we so freely extend to those around us. We need to learn to not be so hard on ourselves, to laugh, to notice and embrace the joyful moments of ministry. In this chapter, we want to look at some of the practical, touching, and perhaps funny moments women have experienced in their ministries, and the grace-full ways they have responded.

It seems baptisms and weddings are ripe with potential for such moments. The first baptism I did, the senior minister offered me the use of his waders. (You should know that I had been absent the day we practiced baptism in seminary—and what a day to miss! So this kind older minister spent an afternoon with me in the baptistry before the big day, giving me the chance to practice, and pointers like, "You need to wear some waders.") In our tradition where we baptize by immersion, it is quite common for ministers to wear waders, those rubber hip boots one wears when fishing. It keeps you dry so you can get back and continue the service as quickly as possible. Well, it was a fine offer, but he was over six feet tall and skinny as a rail, and I'm…well, I'm not. I have a more than generous figure, with plenty of feminine curves. I like to call my body type Rubenesque, as he loved to paint women with the same type of body I have.

Well, it came time for the baptism, and my feminine hips did not fit into those waders cut for a man's physique. Now *there* is an issue for women in ministry! Where do you get waders with hips?! I have asked a couple of others if I could try on their waders since then, but now I have resigned myself to becoming very adept at changing out of wet clothes quickly.

Rev. Susie Cameron, who pastors a church in central Indiana, laughs as she notes that the waders at her church are taller than she is (she is about five feet tall), so it is out of the question for her to use them. She says, "In our new baptistry, I think maybe my head and shoulders might show above the top, but that's probably all, it's that deep. If I baptize any children, we're in trouble."[1] Women are generally of smaller build than men, so we sometimes have to make adjustments with church and chancel furnishings, especially if we have trouble seeing over the pulpit! We might need a stepping stool behind the pulpit, in the baptistry, or some other inconvenient place. Or we might just have to resign ourselves to just peeping over a pulpit built for someone taller.

Rev. Cameron also says it's funny when she goes out with a group of people from her church, and they introduce her as the pastor. She says there's a look of shock on the faces of those she is introduced to that amuses her. She says, "I get a kick out of that because I'm the least likely one there (to be the pastor)." Sometimes women, especially small, diminutive women, have to accept the surprise of others with such good grace as Susie does. It is gift to be able to experience such moments with amusement instead of offense.

Another pastor, Rev. Geneal Wilson,[2] when asked what funny moments she had experienced, tells about an older man who came to be baptized. Unfortunately, he did not tell her until they were in the baptistry that he was afraid of water. She laughed as she said, "This is a fine time to tell me!" She quickly told him, "Fine, you're going forward!" and she baptized him going forward. But that is one of those instances that you just have to "wing it," and adjust to the circumstances.

Geneal also smiled as she confessed, "I almost drowned my son!" It seems that when she was baptizing him, the water was particularly cold. He was twenty years old at the time. He had wanted to reconcile in his own understanding how a loving God could allow his Son to die before he would consent to being baptized. Maybe he carried the weight of that "baggage" with him as his mother, the minister, baptized him. When he went down, he gasped at the water being so cold—just as he was going into the water! After he inhaled the

---

[1]Rev. Susie Cameron, pastor at East Lynn Christian Church, Anderson, Indiana.
[2]Rev. Geneal Wilson, pastor at Strasburg Christian Church, Strasburg, Virginia.

waters of his baptism, she managed to get him back out. But she still smiles as she tells the story, and she says he always likes to refer to his baptism as the day his mother almost drowned him. These are the kind of stories that are told over and over until they become part of the family lore. Such moments shared in families are even more precious when the minister is mom, grandma, wife, sister, or aunt. I personally look forward to the day I get to baptize my nephew and niece, and perhaps even officiate at their weddings.

Speaking of family lore, the first wedding I ever presided at was my cousin's wedding, while I was still in seminary. I was flattered and touched to be asked. I have an uncle who is quite a character, and he apparently did not know what I was going to school for, or that I would be doing the service. When we got there, I walked up to him with my mother, and she asked, "Hey there, you want to give the minister a hard time?" He responded eagerly, "Yeah, let's go give him hell!" At which point I stepped up and said, "Hi!" My mother said, "Well, here's the minister!" The look on his face was priceless, and I don't recall him ever getting around to giving me "hell" yet!

That experience also illustrated for me early on that sometimes our families, however much they love and support us, do not know quite what to do with us as ministers. It is the old story of the prophet being without honor in his (or her!) own home. Our families have long memories, and sometimes have trouble seeing us in a position of authority and leadership in the church. My father called me Rev. Doodles (a childhood nickname) every now and then; my sister laughed about her "little sister, the preacher"; and my mother tended to show me off as a novelty, or mention my ministry as the latest of my cute little antics, like when I was a toddler. You might want to allow your family time to make the transition from seeing you as daughter/sister/wife/mother to minister. They have memories of you as a child in a Christmas play, or eating glue in Sunday school. They know you in your most personal, and perhaps least saintly, moments. As with all families, they hold your history. Try not to let them limit your present and future, though.

I also learned that sometimes you need to be a family member, not a minister, and let someone else do that job. My own wedding involved four ministers in the ceremony: my husband, myself, and the two ministers who co-officiated. One was pastor of my home church; the other was our seminary professor whose class we met in, and who was particularly dear to both of us. When you are both ministers and all your friends at seminary are ministers, it is a challenge to find that special person to marry you. In spite of all these ministers, and the fact that the groom's family traditionally hosts the rehearsal dinner, somehow I got the job of saying the blessing! With all these ministers running around (as well as a handful of church elders), you'd think I could have had the day off! I resented it somewhat because I was the bride, and that is what I wanted to be that day. I didn't want to have to be the minister, too.

As a woman in ministry, at times you will need to allow yourself to be daughter/sister/wife/mother, etc. Sometimes you will be the one who will have to set the boundaries. One time I preached the homily at my cousin's funeral. She was the next one after me in birth order among the cousins, about a year younger, and the mother of a five-year-old son. I could remember sharing her Mrs. Beasley doll when we were children. The last time I had seen her was at my wedding just two months before.

Needless to say, it was one of the most difficult funeral homilies I have ever given. I managed to get through it, until the last phrase, that beautiful passage from the first chapter of John, which says, "What has come into being in him was life, and the life was the light of all people. The light shines in the darkness, and the darkness did not overcome it" (Jn. 1:3b–4). I began to cry, thinking of this beautiful life that had been cut short. On the ride to the cemetery, I told my parents, my sister, and husband I would not do that for them. Someone else would do the homily at their funerals. Sometimes we need to set boundaries, and sometimes those boundaries might exclude us from being pastor when we need to be a family member. When you are involved as a minister in a family event, allow yourself the ability to be a family member too. You may laugh, you may cry, and that's OK.

When I did a chaplaincy residency, we had a lovely resident whose name was Estelle. She was Roman Catholic and a lay minister. She was a French Canadian with a beautiful heart and sensitivity. She once said something that stayed with me, "Let the tears come, they are a gift." As much as we like to be stoic and composed, sometimes it is better to be human and involved. I found that to be true when I was doing the funeral of a dear family friend. As I gave the homily, I got choked up and had to pause a few moments before going on. I'm sure those present could see the emotion in my face, as well as hear it as my voice broke. Sitting there was the pastor of my home church, as well as the regional minister for that area (also a former pastor of my home church)! I was embarrassed that I wasn't being more professional. After the service, a friend came to me and said, "That was the most beautiful tribute you could have given her, because it showed how much you cared." Now, I am not saying that every service should be an expression of our own grief or emotion—that does not suit our calling as a leader or minister to those we serve. But allowing ourselves to express human warmth as well as professionalism is a talent many women possess.

In addition to baptisms and weddings, communion services can bring moments of unexpected joy as well. In my first position out of seminary, I was an associate pastor in a church with four youth groups, where the ages ranged from four years old through high school. Our high school and junior high groups participated in the World Vision 30 Hour Planned Famine. This is a great program where the kids fast for 30 hours, while learning about world hunger and participating in some local hunger relief project. It brings together education, action, and experience. By the end of the 30 hours, though, teenagers do get mighty hungry (and grumpy, and listless!).

We always ended our Famine with a brief communion service before our "break-fast" (a meal, usually pizza, that broke our fast the evening of the second day). The kids showed proper restraint and reverence during the communion service, for which I had gotten King's Hawaiian Bread as a special treat. If you have never had it, it is a nice, sweet bread, soft and quite delicious. After the last amen, though, the kids descended on the rest of that loaf of bread like a flock of hungry birds. It was gone in two minutes flat, if that. I have rarely seen anyone eat with such gusto! What makes me smile still is remembering how enthusiastically they "partook of the elements." I wish we would approach every communion meal that way—with hungry, starving souls, and parched, dry spirits, consuming the bread and the cup with as much enthusiasm as hungry teenagers at the end of a day and a half of fasting.

Sometimes the funniest moments in ministry just grow out of sharing parishioners' lives. One UCC minister, who has been in the ministry for over seventeen years, has a number of these stories. Once, one of her parishioners learned she was going on vacation, so she ate a grape lollipop, and went to the emergency room (it appeared she had a lack of oxygen). They admitted her and called her pastor to come and see her. Apparently she didn't want her pastor to go on vacation! On another occasion, she accompanied an older parishioner to the orthopedic surgeon, and they were placed in a room with the usual anatomy charts, the one in their room being a male. The old lady took one look, and said, "Well, I guess we'll have to sit here for two hours looking at that naked man!"

Another older lady, who was ninety-three years old, was watching the news. The breaking news was that President Clinton had lifted the ban on gays in the military. She looked at her pastor and asked seriously, "Do you think my neighbors are that way?" Our pastor friend kindly said, "No," as her neighbors were an elderly couple married for decades. The older lady said, "Well, they are very forgetful, and they misplace things." Apparently she was confusing homosexuality with Alzheimer's. You never know what you might hear!

Sometimes the joy of ministry comes with simply sharing the everyday lives of those we minister to, be it in the larger life events such as baptisms, funerals, and weddings, or the more common, everyday events that come with pastoral care. You are certain to find such moments of joy and laughter as you journey with those you have been called to serve. We discover holy humor in the sacred moments of our daily lives and ministries. Look for those moments. Humor helps us to look at ourselves, our image, our ministry, and sometimes changes the way we see ourselves. In seeing our faults and foibles, we embrace a larger and more complete image of ourselves. When we see the humor in a situation, at times it allows us to touch people in new ways. Humor can affect our theology, our spirituality, and can make us better, or at least happier, in our ministry. Holy humor surrounds us! Notice it, and use it!

2

Struggling Creatively to Minister

Because of the generation I (Debra) was born into, at the beginning of my career I thought we were past such issues as gender bias (not to say discrimination against women) in the workplace. I was born in 1969 and am a proud Generation X-er, or Baby Buster as we are sometimes called. I am part of the "Free to Be You and Me" generation (a show I really did watch when I was a kid!). I just assumed the issue of women being able to do whatever job they wanted had already been settled. Never did I doubt that if I wanted to be a minister (or astronaut or surgeon or circus performer) that I could do just that. Both my mother and grandmother were professional women, teachers with Masters degrees. I wondered why my "older sisters" at seminary could be so angry and defensive sometimes. I did not understand why women doing ministry was such an issue.

Unfortunately, I found that not everyone accepts women as ministers. That is a reality we have to deal with as women clergy. Not all Protestants approve of ordaining women; some do so grudgingly, and some simply refuse. While women are ordained in most of the mainline Protestant denominations in the United States, the day that our Catholic sisters or more conservative Protestant colleagues can be fully ordained clergy is still sometime in the future.

If we feel called to the ministry, some of us either have to struggle with our denomination, or find another denomination to call home. We were two weeks into our year-long residency on September 11, 2001. Of all places to be, our group was in the hospital morgue as a part of our orientation when we got the news that the planes had flown into the World Trade Center. We got the command, "Go to your floors." Some of us had to find them first. Needless to say, it was an overwhelming day. As a chaplain, people look to you for answers, for wisdom, trying to make some sense of it all. I found myself watching the news coverage with the patients and nurses, and as much at a loss as they were as to what to say. At the end of this day, Katherine, our supervisor, called us together. We spent an hour or so sorting through our day. She was a pastor to us that day. She was a chaplain to the fledgling chaplains and helped us to process the enormity of the event.

Later, when we were doing mid-unit evaluations, she challenged us to evaluate each other in a creative way, instead of just writing the standard paragraph. One fellow likened us all to trees. I wrote poems for each of my colleagues. Everyone brought something delightful to share, and this was as she intended, I suspect. All of this is to say Katherine was a wonderful pastor, with a vibrant ministry as she supervised CPE students. She is one of the most sensitive, creative, compassionate, and fun people I have met. But Katherine had gone to the Southern Baptist Seminary in Louisville, Kentucky, and was struggling with her denomination. She grew up in the Southern Baptist tradition and didn't want to leave it. But they were becoming so conservative, it was hard for her to stay. Katherine's situation points out that while some women find meaningful ministry to do in spite of opposition from the church, it isn't always easy for them.

Many women have overcome obstacles put in place by tradition, by their families, by our society, and by our theology to become powerful and effective ministers. Most I interviewed spoke with glowing eyes and enthusiastic expressions about the joys of ministry and how they could not imagine doing anything else. Some were second-career ministers, some were mothers and grandmothers, some had waited years and even decades to respond to God's call on their lives. They had such spiritual strength and beauty they could not be kept from their calling.

When asked why they went into the ministry, they speak of the honor of preaching the gospel and pastoring a congregation; of possibilities for creativity; of the opportunity to be present with others at such significant and sacred moments as funerals, weddings, baptisms, and births. They speak with passion about a day when we will enjoy peace and equal rights and justice for all, and how empowering it is to be a part of working toward bringing that day about.

Unfortunately, it seems that while women in medicine, law, education, and other secular jobs have found acceptance more readily, religious vocations are one of the last bastions of the old boy network. While in Christianity, particularly American Christianity, finding women as ministers is more and more common, it is still somewhat unusual. Most people, it seems, are simply more used to men as pastors and are still surprised when they meet a woman pastor. Some faith traditions do not allow women in any positions of leadership and cite scriptural basis for their practices, so it may be understandable when one of their members is unsure or even hostile when meeting a woman pastor. They have never met a woman in the ministry. Even for those of us in mainline Protestant denominations in North America, many people in our own churches have never known a woman who was in the ministry and so are curious, at the very least.

Sad to say, discrimination in hiring and salary practices also exists. In a study done by the Barna Research Group in 2000–2001, they found that just 5 percent of all Protestant senior pastors are women—this in spite of the rise of the number of female graduates from mainline protestant seminaries in the United States, which at some seminaries is 50 percent. While female pastors are much more likely to be seminary trained (86 percent, as opposed to 60 percent of male pastors), they last less time in a given church (three years per pastorate, as compared to almost six years by men), and receive much lower compensation packages.[1]

This has proved true in my own experience. I was surprised during my tenure at my first position out of seminary. One man refused to refer to me as "Reverend" or "Pastor." Instead I was "that girl who works with the kids." I had the required degree, had been ordained, but was still not acknowledged or named as a minister by some. Since then, I have found it quite common for people to be mildly surprised when they call for the pastor and find a woman answering the call. They may be impressed or not, but they are often surprised. Unfortunately, many of my sisters in the ministry can share similar stories of being dismissed and discriminated against.

I thought we were past such issues. I thought that calling, gifts, desire, and talents determine your career path, not what Mom or Grandma was allowed to do. But apparently women doing ministry is still an issue. Barriers remain to be broken down, inequalities to be lessened, attitudes to be changed. I do believe that hopefully, over time, attitudes will change. Already the women who have gone before us have done much good work. The trail has been blazed and clearly marked.

Women are making strides in numbers going into ministry, in churches accepting women as their pastors, in lessening the gap with men in our salaries, and in gaining upper level and administrative positions. I am proud that my denomination, the Christian Church (Disciples of Christ), at its General Assembly in July 2005, became the first mainline denomination that I know of to elect a woman as its leader when Rev. Sharon Watkins became our General Minister and President. More recently, the Episcopal Church in America elected their first female presiding bishop, and that was a historic moment as well. Obviously, much room for

---

[1]Data from www.barna.org. "A Profile of Protestant Pastors in Anticipation of 'Pastor Appreciation Month'" study done in 2001 by the Barna Group, Ltd.

improvement remains for all denominations in that respect. The church can use more women bishops, and in other denominational leadership positions. With tongue firmly in cheek, I sometimes say I am encouraged that since we are all now pretty much in agreement that the earth is round and that we shouldn't own slaves, it gives me hope that someday most people will accept women in ministry as well. It does seem that in the mainline Protestant denominations some of the administrative levels are more intentional about hiring equitable numbers of women and men, so that is encouraging. In many regions in my own church, women are on staff as Regional Ministers or Associate Regional Ministers. Fortunately, the state and national manifestations of the church seem more intentional about hiring women than do the local congregations.

According to the Hartford Institute for Religion Research Web site, their study in 1994 was the largest one ever done of clergywomen in America. They asked how a woman's experience is different from a man's, and what a woman's prospects were for employment, income potential, and job satisfaction. They found at the time that, while women accounted for around 11 percent of clergy in mainline Protestant denominations, they do have greater difficulty finding employment; are more likely to be part-time; and with the same experience, qualifications, denomination, and position as a man, they average 9 percent less in salary.[2]

Unfortunately, I also found this to be true in personal experience. My first position out of seminary as an ordained minister was as an associate pastor for youth and family ministries at a midwestern Disciples of Christ congregation that averaged 200–220 in worship each Sunday. I worked there for seven years, and my ending salary was $29,712 in 2001. A year and a half later, I learned they hired a local man, without a M.Div. degree or ordination, as the associate minister of worship, with a starting salary package of $40,000. Needless to say, I was offended.

---

[2]From www.hartsem.edu, the Hartford Institute for Religion Research, "What percentage of pastors are female?" 1994.

While women may continue to struggle to find appropriate employment and an appropriate salary, the women
clergy I know are also gifted at creating new career paths,
and in being creative in responding to the call God has
placed on their lives. If the churches will not hire them, they
find places and means to do the ministry they are called to
anyway. If ministry positions do not yet exist, some women
create ministries, organizations, and ways to do what they
have been trained for and called to. Women are flexible, by
nature or necessity (I am not sure which) and do not seem
as confined to traditionally defined ministry or career tracks.
Perhaps it is because they are not as accepted in traditional
parish positions, but they do not necessarily follow the
associate pastor to solo pastor of a small church to senior
pastor of a larger church progression considered typical for
parish ministers. For example, a fellow clergy woman in
Virginia, after being in the Search and Call process for over a
year, found that she could fulfill her call at a local counseling
agency. Many women in ministry have found they could
minister effectively as chaplains, pastoral counselors, or
advocates, and answer their call to ministry by working in
one of these fields. However, while women clergy can find
fulfillment outside traditional parish ministries, they should
not be barred or excluded from positions in the church if
that is what they feel called to do. If the church is going
to educate and ordain women, they should hire them for
pastoral ministry in their churches too.

In their study for the Hartford Institute for Religion
(1994), Zikmund, Lummis, and Chang also found 16,321
female clergy in fifteen mainline and conservative Protestant
denominations, which means that 11.47 percent of clergy
in those denominations were female.[3] According to those
numbers, on average one out of ten pastors is a woman.
So it is understandable that having a woman pastor is still
unfamiliar and perhaps uncomfortable for some parishioners.
One has to wonder if someday the percentage of women in

---

[3]Study done by the Hartford Institute for Religion Research by Barbara Brown
Zikmund, Adair Lummis and Patricia Chang, 1994.

ministry will better reflect the actual numbers of men and women in the world, at roughly 50/50, or perhaps reflect the percentage of women in our churches, which is even higher. Maybe then it will no longer be so unusual or surprising to have a woman minister.

The distribution across denominations is, of course, not equal. The more theologically liberal groups such as the Unitarian Universalist Association and the United Church of Christ led in the percentage of female clergy, with 30 percent and 25 percent respectively. Most theologically conservative groups—the Southern Baptist Convention (4 percent), the Free Methodist Church (1 percent), and the Assemblies of God (8 percent)—came in with considerably lower percentages. To round out the list, American Baptist churches had 12 percent female clergy, the Christian Church (Disciples of Christ) had 18 percent, the Church of God (Anderson, Indiana) had 10 percent, the Church of the Brethren had 12 percent, the Church of the Nazarene had 11 percent, the Episcopal Church had 12 percent, the Evangelical Lutheran Church in America had 11 percent, the Presbyterian Church had 19 percent, the United Methodist Church had 15 percent, and the Wesleyan Church had 11 percent.[4] Again, we must wonder if any of the churches will someday reflect the 50/50 percentage of men and women in the general population, or the even higher percentage of women in the pews of the churches they serve.

Many voices contend that women are no different from men when it comes to the work they do, that any differences in personality and temperament are instilled in them and can be just as easily trained out of them. Without getting into the old nature versus nurture argument, let's just say that while women and men have to fulfill the same functions and do the same jobs, it does seem that we do them in different ways. In this book, we do not want to paint with such broad strokes that we gloss over the individual differences in either women or men.

---

[4]Ibid.

Some women are strong, competitive administrators, and men can be gentle and compassionate in their ministry. Each one must be taken as an individual. However, that being said, women do bring their uniquely feminine qualities and characteristics to the job they do, and those should be seen as assets rather than liabilities. We want to look at how being a woman enhances one's ministry and work, and how we can utilize our natural inclinations and abilities to better serve the church and the ministries we are called to.

Men's and women's experience of and in life differ. Whether it is a matter of biology or the baby dolls we are given to play with, most women are nurturers to some degree, more so than men. We tend to take care of others. Women also tend to be more collegial in administration and work by consensus, while men tend to be follow the traditional corporation model more, and tend toward making administrative decisions alone. Women tend to be cooperative. Men tend to be competitive. Again, while there are many individual exceptions to these examples, the fundamental point is that women and men are different. We bring those differences to the ministries we do. These differences should be celebrated as a source of strength for the various ministries of the church.

A tension about these differences rises in the professional world, the church, and even within ourselves as women, though. While we are sometimes uncomfortable or even angry at being seen to be different from our male counterparts (because, I suspect, this has led to discrimination in the past), we also do not want to have to compromise who we are as women. We want to be able to "hang with the boys," particularly in this profession that has been harder for women to break into; but we don't want to have to pretend to be a boy to do so. Again, ministry seems to be one of the last great bastions of the male-dominated professions. But we women want to do our work with integrity and wholeness, to bring our gifts and talents to the table, to be recognized and appreciated as women, instead of having to act like men in skirts.

Women must not be made to feel that they must learn to be and do ministry more like their male colleagues. Far from it; the gifts, traits, and talents women bring to the work they do will greatly enhance and help the church in its mission and ministry. As Paul said, the body is made up of many parts, and all parts are worthy and valuable (1 Cor. 12:12–30). This book is meant to lift up and celebrate those differences and to discover and delight in the different ways women do ministry.

All this women bring to the ministry they do, and not only do we bring our unique gifts and presence, we bring an energy and enthusiasm to ministry, especially those sisters who have known what it is to be denied the opportunity to do the ministry they felt called to. Like a stream bursting through a dam, the energy of women for the work of the church can no longer be denied, and they are making their presence felt.

3

The Sacred Feminine

I (Debra) was born into an American Baptist family (all my grandparents were Baptist, as were my parents), so I was a baby Baptist, and I have the cradle roll certificate to prove it. When I was one year old, we joined the Christian Church (Disciples of Christ), as my mother was a church organist and got a job there. I was raised in that church until I was fifteen. I spent my high school and college years as a United Methodist (again, a job change for mom precipitated the move). When I went to seminary, I moved my membership back to the Christian Church (Disciples of Christ) and was ordained in that denomination. So basically I have a solid, mainline Protestant background. Also, I should tell you I was blessed to be raised in a family with warm and loving parents.

All this is to say, I was not raised with a concept of the sacred feminine in my religious background, nor did I have a problem with the image of God as father. So when I got to seminary and was introduced to feminine images of God, I had the usual reaction: "That's just not necessary!" Yet as time went on, and I studied psychology, archaeology, and theology, I realized there were deep, ancient underpinnings for a concept of the sacred feminine. There was some truth, or at least possibility, there that I had to consider. Too many cultures and peoples have inhabited this planet that conceive of God in feminine form to dismiss it outright. I also came to realize that God is God, and any attempt to confine God to a masculine or father image is simply idolatry. God cannot be confined by our human conceptions.

True, thinking of God in feminine terms is not a strong part of our Judeo-Christian tradition, but there seems to be an undercurrent, a groundswell, that is happening in the world, and in our culture, that cannot be ignored. A good illustration of this is a book that made one of the biggest stirs in recent years, Dan Brown's *The DaVinci Code*. Granted, it is a good murder/mystery novel, with exotic locales, exciting plot twists, and interesting characters. But having read the novel, and some of the follow-up books on "solving" the DaVinci Code, I believe the appeal of the book goes beyond those things. And I think part of the appeal, or source of controversy, has to be the decidedly positive light it casts on Mary Magdalene, the questions it raises about the suppression of her role, and its intriguing advocacy of feminine images of the divine.

Not to give away the plot (but if you haven't read it yet, I doubt you are going to), in Brown's novel, Mary Magdalene is the elusive "Holy Grail" of medieval mythology. The theory goes that she was not a prostitute, as she has been painted to be by some for centuries, but was instead the wife of Jesus Christ, the first among his disciples, and the bearer of his child. She held in her body his royal blood, and thus she was the Holy Grail. She was later defamed and falsely portrayed as a prostitute by the leaders of the church, due to her conflict with the masculine power structure of the early church and their desire to discredit her.

Now while the historical and factual nature of Brown's book may be called into question, as indeed it has been, it seems some of the public backlash against Brown's story was a reaction against a woman being presented so prominently in the Christian religion. Many readers were not ready for a woman to be so important and so closely associated with Jesus. Her connection with Christ was seen as appalling.

The Son of God consorting with a woman seems, in a word, *sordid*. And there seems to be a reluctance to learn about Mary's leadership in the early church. It seems we can barely get our Christian minds around the concept of a woman being, well, so *holy*. This is due to a number of reasons of course: centuries of tradition establishing Christ's celibacy; theological underpinnings denouncing women as a source of evil; the echoes of Greek dualism telling us that such physical pleasure is not appropriate for such a spiritually pure being as Jesus Christ.

It has well been said that the Judeo-Christian tradition is decidedly patriarchal. It is a tradition that has been largely shaped and formed by men. Our scriptures were written by men, mostly about men. Most references to God in both scripture and tradition are masculine. Jesus referred to God as Abba, or Father, so that settles it, doesn't it? Not if you consider that New Testament Christianity grew out of Judaism and the patriarchal Greco-Roman world. And that the Jewish tradition, which Jesus and the earliest disciples were a part of, while giving women rights they did not enjoy elsewhere, was also decidedly patriarchal.

Unfortunately, women have often not fared well in the resulting Christian tradition. For centuries of theology, women were at the very least considered inferior creatures to men. Most theologians held them responsible, through Eve, for the fallen nature of humanity. Eve was responsible for falling prey to the snake's trickery, and by her weakness tempting her husband as well, and so evil entered the world.

In many cases people found support for ignoring women's ministerial gifts by citing 1 Corinthians 14:33b–35: "As in all the congregations of the saints, women should remain silent in the churches. They are not allowed to speak, but must be in submission, as the Law says. If they want to inquire about something, they should ask their own husbands at home; for it is disgraceful for a woman to speak in the church" (NIV).

In an article in *DisciplesWorld*, the denominational magazine of the Christian Church (Disciples of Christ), John Temple Bristow encapsulates the social, cultural, and theological worldviews held by those who wrote our

New Testament scriptures. He notes that most of the early church fathers were schooled in Greek philosophy. In the Greco-Roman world women were thought of as inherently inferior to men. Women were regarded as sexual possessions. Demosthenes acknowledged only three roles for women: as courtesans, prostitutes, or wives. All three were defined in relation to men's sexual pleasure and women's fertility.

Such education encouraged notable men like John Chrysostom to write of women as, "a foe to friendship, an inescapable punishment, a necessary evil, a natural temptation, a desirable calamity, a domestic danger, a detectable detriment, an evil nature, painted with false colors."[1] Some of the Church Fathers were even harsher in their condemnation. Jerome wrote that women were the source of evil, were themselves evil, and should be avoided. Such thinking contributed to centuries of oppression.

In Christianized Europe, women were not allowed to own property, to have leadership positions in society, and were considered to be the property of men, valued only slightly above the livestock and other chattel for the most part. Millions of women—mostly poor, older women who knew about natural and herbal remedies, or women who challenged the men in their world—were duly punished, humiliated, or condemned as witches and either burned or drowned. Church leaders were responsible for publishing such books as *Malleus Maleficarum*, or "Hammer of the Witches" to help identify such deviants. Some estimates put the number of women tortured and killed over two thousand years of Christianity's dominance in Europe as roughly equal to the number of those killed in the Holocaust in Nazi Germany.[2]

Against this dark curtain of history it is no wonder that so many are uncomfortable with women in roles of leadership

---

[1]John Temple Bristow, "Sexual Extremes and the New Testament," *DisciplesWorld*, vol. 4 no. 7, (Sept., 2005) 10–12.

[2]For a discussion of the number, which could be as high as 9–11 million, see Richard J. Green's article "How Many Witches" (www.holocaust.history.org/~rjg/witches.shtml).

in the church. We have centuries of history and tradition in the church working against us. It seems the church has precious few images of women as good, much less sacred, beings. Centuries of teaching have made us understand that women are inferior in intellect, moral fortitude, and spiritual insight. Even women in the ministry are sometimes caught in the tension between what the church has traditionally taught about women and their understanding of themselves as ministers. We are left asking ourselves, what is a couple of decades of empowerment for women in the face of centuries of misogyny?

Women in ministry have a choice. We can accept the status quo of the Christian tradition, but at times this leads us to having to defend our right to do ministry in light of a tradition that historically says we are not intellectually or morally fit to do so. Or, we can recognize the patriarchal nature of the society the church was born into and allow for its influence on our scriptures, our leaders, and the church. We can then choose whether or not we accept that worldview today, or if there has been such a seismic shift in perspective, at least in North American and Western European culture, that we can now see women as equal to men in their ability to do ministry.

Do not misunderstand! For the most part I love our Christian heritage and think our tradition is filled with truth and beauty. I would not be a Christian, much less a minister of our faith, unless I believed in it. But this tradition includes only a scant number of female voices. We women are left looking for female models of leadership as we go about doing our ministry. Our tradition, as much as we love it, does have undercurrents of misogyny, no matter how much we stand against them, or would rather they were not there.

Do not be fooled! These currents run deep and spring up when you least expect them. On Easter 2006, I had finished my service at my church and gone to my husband's church, where the service was at a later time. They had a guest pianist for the cantata that day, and I was introduced to him as "the pastor's wife, the *other* Rev. Harmon." I joked that when people called our home and asked for Rev. Harmon, they had to specify which one they wanted. The young man (not old, mind you, but in his twenties!), said, "Yeah, well, I suppose they would be expecting a man if they asked for a Reverend, wouldn't they?" I was taken by surprise. Later reflection allowed me to realize how far we have yet to go before women are considered as equally legitimate ministers.

While it might feel a bit like swimming upstream, I believe women in ministry benefit and are strengthened spiritually by finding sacred images that respect and celebrate the female half of the human experience. To do so is to validate their own experience, to support and empower themselves as women leaders of the church, and also to help change feelings and attitudes within the church. It may feel awkward, or seem a bit extreme. You might be thinking, "I am perfectly comfortable with my ministry and consider myself a fully legitimate member of the clergy. I do not need to rewrite our history and tradition." However, when you realize the strength of the history and tradition that dismiss us as women ministers, it seems we would do well to have some strong images of the sacred feminine.

Again, referring to my own journey, I have found myself strengthened and uplifted by conceptualizing God in feminine form. We have strains of this in our tradition if we look for them, and it allows us as women to participate in the divine, to see ourselves as holy. It legitimizes our ministry. It also speaks to our spirits as women.

Think about it. When was the last time you heard a sermon or a prayer in a church that made you feel good about being a woman? We refer to God as Father without a thought, but to refer to God as Mother makes most of us feel a bit odd, and we worry how our congregations would respond. My husband and I were doing a program for a district men's meeting and wanted to do a skit of a conversation with God. He thought it would be interesting to cast me in the role of God. Quite a discussion ensued between us about how the men would react to a woman in the role of God, whether they would laugh, would be offended, or not think a thing about it. We were too concerned it would cause offense and detract from the skit, so we eventually cast my husband as

God (although I put the words into God's mouth, as I wrote the skit!).

While the liturgy of the church and some translations of the Bible are becoming more inclusive, it remains a sticking point for many congregations how inclusive they want to be. One of the major battlegrounds where this issue is fought is around the subject of the hymns we sing. Many of us object to the words of older, dearly loved hymns being changed for the purpose of inclusiveness. Fortunately, we are seeing more newer hymns of the church that refer to God in female terms, or at least bring other images of God in addition to father. Committees that have compiled recent hymnals have been intentional about including a wider variety of images of God. For example, the *Chalice Hymnal*, my denomination's current hymnal, includes "Bring Many Names," "God of Many Names," "Womb of Life, Source of Being," "Creator God, Creating Still," "How Like a Gentle Spirit," "The Care the Eagle Gives Her Young," and "Mothering God, You Gave Me Birth." The challenge is, of course, to teach our congregations to accept and sing these newer hymns.

Women ministers handle the issue of God-talk in different ways. Rev. Geneal Wilson, a Disciples of Christ pastor, says, "I do try to lift up feminine images that are found in scripture. I try to reword all of my language so I don't have to use masculine. I do not tend to substitute feminine for masculine. There are occasions when that has been appropriate, but by and large that is not the way I've chosen to go. I've chosen to rework the language whenever possible." But she cautions, "I guess I just find that if it's not done well, it sets up more resistance and puts up some barriers. If it isn't done well, they don't even hear anything after that. But I do find you can use more of that with the younger generation that with older congregations. The reality is that in most of our congregations, the majority are a bit older, although obviously that's changing."[3]

---

[3]Rev. Geneal Wilson, pastor at Strasburg Christian Church, Strasburg, Virginia.

Rev. Barbara Rhodes, my coauthor, says that she is intentional about including inclusive language and images of God for her congregations. She says one of her favorite images to use, especially in prayer, is the biblical image of being enfolded under God's wings, and protected in God's arms. Both of these are decidedly feminine images, at least as they are used in biblical settings. But she says she has also experienced her share of joking resistance. At one of her churches, they were rehearsing for a play. She noticed that the word *mankind* was used repeatedly. She asked that they use the more inclusive *humankind* wherever that occurred. That request made her the resident authority on inclusive language. As they continued to practice the play, members repeatedly asked her if a line was inclusive enough. While they might have meant it as a joke, she experienced it as some underlying resistance to her request for more inclusive language.

Another Disciples pastor, Rev. Susie Cameron, when asked about using feminine images of the sacred, says:

> I don't really think about it. I had never thought about it until I went to seminary, of course. The first time I heard about thinking about God as mother, I had never thought of that, and I'm fine with that... Do I go out of my way to look for it? No. Would I make a big deal of it at my church? No. I guess I am probably pretty comfortable with the old religion. I don't have a problem with that. I don't see God as Grandpa or Grandma, either one... My congregation is mostly elderly; they would be really uncomfortable. Making them uncomfortable is not my job.[4]

So there is discomfort and resistance. Ministers have to think very practically as to whether or not the gender issue is a battle they want to take on, especially when they are employed by a congregation. Some ministers find subtle

---

[4]Rev. Susie Cameron, pastor at East Lynn Christian Church, Anderson, Indiana.

ways to integrate more balanced language. Some see it as a battle they would rather not fight.

To add another caveat: for some of our parishioners, God-as-Father might not be a positive image. Many books about this are available. If you had any pastoral counseling classes in seminary, you probably read some of them. One minister friend made the observation that it was not an issue for her. Blessed to grow up with a loving father, it never occurred to her that God-as-Father was not a warm, comforting image. Then she realized that for some people who have experienced abuse or neglect, who have had a father who is absent, angry, harsh, or violent, this is not a helpful image of God. We do not want to communicate to people that God will violate, manipulate, or abuse them. Of course, some will say that victims of abuse should be able to distinguish between their human father and a Heavenly Father. Perhaps on an intellectual level they can. But as a student of pastoral care and counseling, I wonder if they can make that differentiation on a gut, emotional level. And should we ask them to? Or could we perhaps offer other, less traumatic images of God, in an attempt to include all our parishioners under the sheltering wings of the Almighty?

In addition to helping our churches use more inclusive and feminine images for God, another issue for us as women ministers is how we manage to integrate our gender into our leadership roles, including our understanding of the divine. It requires more effort for women, as we are not readily handed images such as men are. They have God the Father, and Christ the Son, and the twelve disciples to draw from for inspiration. Most of the heroes of scripture are just that—heroes, not heroines. From childhood we are told stories of Noah, Moses, and David; Abraham, Isaac, and Jacob; Peter, Paul, and John. Rarely are we given stories in which women are the examples of faith, notable exceptions being Ruth and Esther in the Hebrew Scriptures, and Mary the mother of Jesus and Mary Magdalene in the New Testament.

Now you might be thinking, "Why do we need feminine images of the sacred? I'm just fine with God the Father. I don't need or want any female goddess. It isn't a part of my faith anyway." Perhaps not, but doesn't it at least bother you that the female half of humanity has been denigrated by our tradition, and even by members of our churches, simply because of their gender? Don't you think our tradition should affirm the other half of humanity? And what do you do with being a woman and trying to preach texts from the Bible that are patently degrading to women? For example, what do you do with the concubine in Judges 19:1—20:7, who is gang raped and then sawn apart by her master? Do you ignore it and pretend that it is not there? What about Hagar (Gen. 21:8–20), who is used and then sent away with her son into the desert at the whim of Abraham, who is supposed to be her protector? What of the way Bathsheba is used by the "hero" King David, made a widow, and then taken as one of David's wives, with apparently no choice in the matter (2 Sam. 11:1–27)? Or what of David's own daughter, Tamar, who was raped by her brother, and for whom we don't hear a word of defense from her father David (2 Sam. 13:1–20)? What do we do with these stories as women ministers?

If not for the sake of your own faith journey, what of the people you minister to? Are you comfortable with a tradition that some of them use to oppress and even abuse their wives and girlfriends, because "the Bible says it"? Do you want to teach our daughters and sons that women are still just a little less than men, a rib, an afterthought, or do you want them to see women as having the same status as men in our religious tradition?

To see women as sacred requires an almost seismic shift in worldview for some people. But we can find sacred feminine images in Christianity, if we look hard enough. It might not be as hard as expected. First of all, female images for God appear in our scriptures (yes, right there in our very own Bible!). In Deuteronomy 32:11, Moses refers to God when he says, "As an eagle stirs up its nest, / and hovers over its young; / as it spreads its wings, takes them up, / and bears them aloft on its pinions." In Psalm 17:8, David asks God to, "Guard me as the apple of the eye; / hide me in the shadow of your wings." This is a feminine image of God, that of a mother protecting her young.

Also, in the Proverbs and Ecclesiastes, when referring to wisdom as something to be greatly desired and sought after, the term used is Sophia, which is a feminine personification of wisdom.

Another thing to consider is that the third of the Ten Commandments says, "You shall not make for yourself an idol, whether in the form of anything that is in heaven above, or that is on the earth beneath, or that is in the water under the earth" (Ex. 20:4; see, too, Deut. 5:8). God is spirit; God is love. If we cannot conceive of God in any other form than that of a human male, we are making an idol of men. This to me is the most compelling argument for considering and using feminine images of the Divine: that if we can only see God as male, we are raising the male image to Godlike status, and that is idolatry. Mary Daly wrote, "If God is male, then male is God."[5] If we share in that thinking then we are limiting God and our understanding of God.

If you haven't already done so, try to write a sermon or paper without referring to God in the masculine form. If you are a layperson, try praying a prayer without referring to God in masculine terms. Hard, isn't it? It is so ingrained in us that it is challenging and uncomfortable to do otherwise. This is the strength of the tradition we are up against. That is why we need to access feminine images of God, to counter this tendency, to guard against idolatry, and to build up our understanding of this being we worship, God.

Not only do we find feminine images for God in the scriptures, human women can be seen in a different light as well. Publishers have issued a number of excellent feminist commentaries in the past few decades. It helps us as women to read them. For example, if you read the priestly creation story in Genesis 1, you will find that women were created simultaneously with men. "So God created humankind in his image, / in the image of God he created them; / male and female he created them" (Gen. 1:27). So woman, too, is created in God's image. Logically, then, if we can conceive of

---

[5]Mary Daly, *Beyond God the Father: Toward a Philosophy in Women's Liberation* (Boston: Beacon Press, 1973), 19.

a male God, then certainly we can conceive of a female God! OK, you say, but Genesis chapter 2 clearly says woman was made from the rib of a man to be his helper (Gen. 2:20–23). Yes, it does say that. But do you also know that the word used for "helper" is most often used for God, as in "the Lord is my helper" (Heb. 13:6; cf. Ps. 13:6)? So we are in some pretty powerful company as helpers of men, aren't we, girls?

For those of us who are willing to step outside our Christian tradition, other sacred feminine images can inspire us. One of the gifts of our postmodern worldview is that we can affirm that which is good and true in other traditions as well as our own. In that light, finding religious traditions that have images of the sacred feminine can be helpful. In her book, *The Chalice and the Blade*, Riane Eisler traces the history of the goddess back to the most ancient of cultures. In the Paleolithic and Neolithic cultures, they venerated the goddess as the source of life and fertility. In such civilizations as Crete between 6000 B.C.E. and 2000 B.C.E., the goddess was worshiped, characterized by peace, arts, and beauty. A love of life and nature was evident in the worship of the goddess.[6]

Other traditions that have strong goddess figures are Wicca and Hindu. In the Hindu faith, Shakti is a powerful goddess of primal energy. In Wicca, and other neo-pagan religions, the goddess, most often associated with the moon, is often venerated.

If this is bordering on heretical for you, or if you would rather not access images of the divine outside of our Judeo-Christian tradition, remember the larger point is that, as women, it helps *us* to find images that strengthen us as women and as leaders of our faith tradition. We need to know in the depths of our souls that we are good, and holy, and loved. We need to see examples of women who were strong leaders. We need to show our daughters (and sons!), not to mention the congregations whose spiritual lives we are responsible for, those images and examples as well.

---

[6]Riane Eisler, *The Chalice and the Blade* (San Francisco: HarperSanFrancisco, 1987), 30–31.

Let us not forget the women of the Bible who managed to shine through the masculine writing and editing. Of course, my favorite is Deborah, the prophetess and judge found in Judges 4—5, whose name I share. She was a wise leader of her people, and Barak would not go into battle until Deborah agreed to go with him! A number of brave and faithful women join her in scripture: Sarah, Rebekah, Leah, Rachel, Ruth, Rahab, Huldah, and Esther. The fathers of Israel certainly could not have done their work without the mothers of Israel by their side!

In the New Testament, we have the women disciples: Mary Magdalene, Joanna, Salome, and others, who followed and supported Jesus along with the men. These women were brave enough to follow him to the cross, when all the men had betrayed, deserted, or fled from Jesus. They also had the joy of being the first to see the resurrected Jesus. All four gospels agree that Mary Magdalene (along with some of the other women?) was the first to witness the resurrection. Jesus spent time at the home of Mary and Martha, and shared a close relationship with them. Paul speaks of Lydia and Phoebe as partners in the gospel, and these women supported him in his ministry.

Of course, the most striking representative of the sacred feminine in the New Testament is Mary, the mother of Christ. She embodies ancient archetypes of the virgin and the mother. Catholics have venerated her, almost to the level of an equal status with her son. In her we see a reminder of the sacred mother of other, earlier religions, and we celebrate the life-giving power of women. All of these women encourage us as women of faith today.

Women have shone as paragons of faith, often against great odds, in the history of Christianity. Queens and saints, nuns and mystics have lived lives of faith and mission. In seminary my husband took a class on the women mystics of medieval Europe, and so now I have the benefit of all the books he acquired for that course! If you have never heard about or studied any of these women, I encourage you to do so. Some of the most prominent among them were Teresa of Avila, Catherine of Genoa, Julian of Norwich, Hildegard of Bingen, Mechthild of Magdeburg, Beatrice of Nazareth, Hadewijch of Antwerp, and Marguerite Porete. These women ranged from abbesses of convents, to having ecstatic visions that informed their spiritual lives; from writing theology, often conversing with great theologians we have studied in seminary, to living lives of quiet piety and devotion. They were administrators, teachers, spiritual guides, and prophetic voices. They were our spiritual ancestors as women ministers.

I encourage you to look at your own denomination and find modern women who opened the way for you to pursue your calling within your tradition. In the Christian Church (Disciples of Christ), Clara Hale Babcock is cited as being the first woman ordained as a minister, and she began her ministry in 1888. Today, the women clergy of our denomination as a group are called the "Daughters of Clara," in honor of her. Other women have forged the path before us. Get to know women who have been in ministry twenty, thirty, forty, or more years. Hear their stories. Be inspired. They have much to teach us.

While this may be a largely theological and philosophical issue, it does impact women, and women who are called to the ministry especially. If you are a woman in ministry, where do you find images that support and sustain you, that allow you to be fully feminine and fully a minister? Have you experienced a negative impact from living and working in a predominantly patriarchal tradition? Has your work and ministry suffered because of it? Have you ever felt challenged, dismissed, or degraded due to your gender? If you are a colleague, a friend, a family member, or a congregant of a woman minister, can you see how these issues might impact her ministry?

Knowing that we are facing at least two thousand years of patriarchal culture and tradition, we of course must realize that it will take time to transform our faith and our culture. Women have been in the active, ordained ministry in the United States for just over one hundred years now, though not in any significant numbers until much more recently. We still have a way to go before we are fully accepted and affirmed in our ministry. It may take at least another generation or two for that to fully come about. For now we need an awareness of the issue and a commitment to finding images of the sacred feminine to support and encourage us. We need to do this both in our own personal devotional lives and also as a service to the wider faith community that we serve.

How do we go about finding images of the sacred feminine and utilizing them in our own thinking, reading, studying, and praying? You can look to some of the examples named earlier. If you feel comfortable looking outside the Judeo-Christian tradition, you can research some of the other religions that have a strong goddess image. Try praying to God our Mother, Creatrix of the Universe, sometime—focusing on the feminine power of producing life, or the tender nurturing of a Mother's hand. You can pursue Sophia, the feminine embodiment of wisdom, found especially in the wisdom literature of Proverbs and Ecclesiastes. Realize how much time and effort you have offered at her shrine as you earned your degree, taught classes, and prepared your sermons.

In the communities of faith we serve, we can be as intentional as we want about including feminine images of the divine in our prayers, meditations, and in our worship. But don't just spring it on them! That will produce more resistance than assistance. If you choose to take this on, and help your congregants explore other images of God, explain why you are using these terms, point to biblical precedents, and explain the theology. Give a little lesson in history and philosophy, so they can understand why we've gotten to where we are. Most of us were introduced later to these concepts; we weren't raised with them. Remember how you felt when first introduced to God as Mother, and allow your congregants some time to adjust and take it in as well. Likewise, as we educate our parishioners (and others!), we need remember they, too, have centuries of tradition at work in their minds and may never be receptive to the concept of the sacred feminine.

But for their sakes, for the sakes of those who come after us, and most especially, for the sake of our own spiritual strength and professional integrity, let's consider integrating the image of the sacred feminine into our own thinking and being. It may be the most important issue we as women in ministry deal with, and the greatest gift we have to give the faith community we serve.

4

Unique Challenges for Women in Ministry

We meet with many challenges every day as women. Mine started when I (Barbara) was a little girl. I was challenged by a neighbor boy to play "Superman" and jump off a high wall just like he did. He said I could do this if I wore his Superman cape. Now, he was five years older than me, yet I decided to meet his challenge and put on the cape, but it was not a safe trip down for me. I fell on my face and had to be taken to the hospital for stitches. This was the last time I was allowed to play with "Superman." However, as I grew up, other challenges were placed before me. Later in life I discovered the challenges involved with wearing a robe and a stole. In this chapter we will talk about the unique challenges for women in ministry.

With Christ, I always felt everyone is equal. I grew up believing this because it is what my parents taught me. When I was four years old, we lived beside a church parsonage. My mother told me I could play with the minister's daughter. My mother watched me as I made my way through our yard and theirs. She saw me knock on the front door. Shortly afterward, she saw the door open. I came home screaming. I could not tell her what was going on. She picked me up and took me right back over to the parsonage. This time when the door opened at our knock, it was the minister's wife. My mother explained to her what happened. The minister's wife was shocked. Then someone appeared behind her.

I began to scream again.

She laughed and said, "Moses must have answered the door. He is a missionary from Africa who is staying with us."

It was the first time I had seen an African, someone with black skin. My mother took me into the house, and we sat with Moses and talked. He took me on his lap and said, "God made us both. We have the same color of blood. My skin is a different color because of where I came from. God makes us all different but loves us all the same."

From that moment on, I thought we were all equal in God's sight. And I then naïvely drew from this that we were also equal in *each other's* sight.

Sometimes just being a woman is a challenge. One time, the challenge was present, and I did not even realize it was. When I was in seminary, a professor gave me a difficult time. All research papers I wrote were incorrect. He told me to do them over. Each time he told me what he wanted. I did it his way; however, it was still wrong.

One day, a fellow student stopped by my desk when I was in the library. He told me, "You know what is wrong, don't you? You have three strikes against you: you are a woman, you are a woman in the ministry, and you are a woman minister in the United Church of Christ." From that moment on, I knew many—even well-educated—church members and leaders held prejudice against women in the ministry. I accepted this and moved on. I did not look for it, but I recognized it when it came and dealt with it. I realized there will always be prejudice. People can be prejudiced against anything. You just have to keep being yourself and being true to yourself, and keep the faith.

When I was looking for a church, my profile was sent to the church where I was eventually hired as pastor. For one year my profile sat on their desk along with sixty others. Members of the search committee later told me that as they went through the profiles, mine kept coming to the top. They kept putting it on the bottom because I was a woman. Their tradition was long pastorates with men. Finally, one gentleman on the search committee said, "We need to look at her profile because it keeps coming to the top." They finally did and eventually called me as a pastor, a position I served in for nine years.

Susie Cameron describes some of her experiences:

It had gotten as far as my going to meet the board. I had been told it was a rubber stamp. So I went to the board meeting. I left, and they said they would call me as soon as the vote. I was on my way back to Lexington. I had my cell phone. I knew something was the matter when I had not heard from them in over an hour. Come to find out a man on the search committee (I should never have gotten as far as I did) actually was against a woman period. So that was a very painful process because it should never have gotten that far. They hadn't done their homework right. It should have been a unanimous vote of the search committee to get to the board. So that was one of the biggies.

The other one I experienced a year ago. I had been invited to the mayor's prayer breakfast. First of all, I walked in beside the mayor, whom I had never met. He didn't know me from a hole in the wall, but he never spoke to me or anyone. We walked in, and I said, "Hello"; but he didn't say anything to me. Completely silent all the way in the door, down the hall. We get to the table where they're registering people, and he puts on his politics hat and just gushes over these girls at the table. He had not said a word to me. So that set me off at the beginning. Then I sat at a table with all men. I think it might have been verbally said, "Isn't it nice that the little woman is the pastor?" So they were very condescending. I was really uncomfortable.[1]

We know prejudice of women in leadership roles will always exist. Some church members will not believe in women pastors because of such prejudice. It doesn't matter if it is ministry, or any vocation where a woman would be in a leadership role over a man. Others feel "a woman should be silent in church." Women are challenged to prove themselves worthy of the calling of God. Often I have quoted Acts 2:17 to someone who openly opposes women in the ministry, "I will pour out my Spirit upon all flesh, / and your sons and your daughters shall prophesy." We cannot argue with God's call to us. God calls each of us to minister in some way. Usually, I do not go out of my way to overtly try to convince people since many already are fixed in their belief. When teachable moments occur, I take the opportunity to state my case. I also have found that people may use some scriptures to oppose women, yet other scriptures prohibiting sin do not bother these same people. Some of the things they do are very sinful, and yet the scriptures concerning these issues are overlooked. On two separate occasions and in two different churches in my ministry, two men who would not attend church because I was a woman minister did not have a problem having sex out of marriage and impregnating church members they were dating.

Geneal Wilson said she does not find discrimination in the congregation generally:

> You might have one, but that's not a general thing. I do find discrimination less now than when I first started in the ministry, but it is still there in ecumenical settings, in community settings. It's a little less pronounced than it was twenty years ago. It's still there. The congregation still has to deal with it. In a

---

[1]Rev. Susie Cameron, pastor at East Lynn Christian Church, Anderson, Indiana.

sense the congregation deals with it more than I have to because of people in the workplace. I remember very well when I was doing that interim, I had people come and say, "You know, we don't believe this, but we don't know how to respond. People are telling us we're going to hell because we've let our children have a woman minister and that's against scripture." I've still found that. I've had a couple people even here, family members who say those things about going to hell, or they just don't believe in it. Actually, they deal with it more than I do.

When you get in an ecumenical setting, they just kind of ignore you. Nobody is nasty. The reality is most people that are talking that way with that kind of language are not open to discussion. So there are a limited number of things you can really say. I guess some of the education that goes on is more informal than formal. It says, "Okay here are the scriptures that you can cite as your authority from scripture." But I just tell them, there's no point in going head to head, thinking you're going to change their minds, because you're not. But for your sense of knowing and authority on it, here are the scriptures I found that have validated my calling."[2]

Another challenge is understanding that we see things differently than do men and, in fact, than do other women. Each of us is born with different skills and knowledge. I have the gift of wisdom in seeing things the way they can be done even when others do not. For instance, when everyone in the congregation had given up on having a Christmas dinner in our church fellowship hall because it would not seat everyone, I showed them another way. Of course, they only saw one way of placing the tables. I tried to explain to them how I envisioned it, and how it would work. The only way to prove my point was to place the tables the way I envisioned. They saw it would work. They stood there

---

[2]Rev. Geneal Wilson, pastor at Strasburg Christian Church, Strasburg, Virginia.

watching as I started to do this. Finally, when they saw it would work, they joined in helping me. It has been sixteen years, and it is still working.

I have been a part of a clergy Bible study since I have been serving churches. As we study the Bible, we have conversations about it. I have noticed how differently men and women think. Of course, God reveals things to each of us, but sometimes it is a challenge to make members of the opposite sex understand your way of thinking. They look at you as if you are from another planet. I have noticed that, as we talk about planning worship, ideas are different. It is good to listen to one another. You can learn how someone else's thinking process works, and you may get some ideas. The educational process to help others understand your ministry is a challenge. Ann Graves, an interim minister, says her greatest frustration has been the sense that somehow the church does not take interim ministry seriously. She says:

> It has been a long educational process, and because I move around so much, it has been hard to be seen as a "regular" participant in the life of the wider church, such as in associations. They often don't quite know what to do with me. In many aspects, I've had to find my own way. Being ordained for interim ministry was difficult in the first place. I was the first in my association. I am usually not considered for executive committees and church and ministry committees—perhaps they're not sure where I'll be next. I also feel that I have had to fight for the same benefits and financial considerations that settled pastors received. However, the church has come a long way over the past ten years, and it is getting much better, as intentional interim ministry is now being recognized as important to the church. The last three interims have paid me on the same basis as their settled pastors were.[3]

---

[3]Rev. Ann Graves, interim pastor, State College, Pennsylvania.

The educational process is a challenge to us and a gift of opportunity. There are teachable moments available to us to help bring understanding and to further Christ's mission in the world. These teachable moments are in the church and the community where we serve. It may take a simple moment, or it may take years.

I found when I first went into the ministry that one of the biggest challenges was dealing with other women—especially, women my age. When I was in seminary, I was serving at a Christian Education Meeting in our association of churches. A lady blew up at me about my talking about seminary. She was very hostile toward me. I could not understand what she was really trying to say so I went to visit her later. In our conversation, I learned that she had wanted to do the same thing that I was doing, except she could not because of finances and the health of her spouse. She was jealous that I was able to pursue my dream and my calling. It is very interesting how things work out. Several years later, I was leading a women's seminar. In the closing worship service we all joined in a circle following communion, and this same lady ended up next to me. We all joined hands and sang, "Bind Us Together." Afterward, we shared a time together, talking about her future. God is working things out if we just listen and wait.

In the church, some women find you a challenge and a competition to them. Humility and caring helps to bridge relationships. This does not always make a win/win situation, but it helps. I found it did not help in one situation. I met these two women who challenged my faith and beliefs. They did not want to learn from me, but rather to see if I believed the same way they did. They were women of faith but felt threatened by another woman of faith. They finally went to other churches. It was all right for them to go where they felt comfortable, and where others believed the way they did. It did not mean that any of us was wrong in our thinking, but that we were different. It is a challenge to believe that not everyone is going to love us and accept our teaching and beliefs. After all, many people rejected Jesus.

Dealing with disappointment and rejection offers a challenge. Tresa Quarles tells about her greatest frustration and disappointment in ministry: "To give heart and soul to a job for twelve years that ended in my resignation was a great disappointment." Tresa served a small rural church where for years two families had struggled for power. As in so many small churches there are these struggles. The congregation had gone through many tough times. They had two splits and a murder; the church burned down; and the main leader of the church died. What a challenge to minister to a congregation who had gone through all of these trials and tribulations. What had been a vital ministry ended badly with hostility and disappointment. These were turned against her. It is sad. It is a challenge to deal with rejection and disappointment. Healing is needed for all, and it takes time. But it happens, and all move on. On this sad day for Tresa, she expressed her faith even about her resignation and disappointment, "The Lord set my feet upon a rock."[4]

Ann Graves shares,

> In the most difficult interim I have undertaken, I was ministering to a congregation that experienced severe pastoral misconduct and knew that I would not survive if I didn't seek outside help and support. Those were the three most intense years I have spent in ministry, because it was also my home congregation. Those years also represented my greatest achievement. During the three years I was there, they ran two capital campaigns and did a 1.2 million [dollar] renovation of the church building. That's one way to recover from pastoral misconduct!
>
> We face many challenges we must deal with as women in the ministry. We cannot do it alone. We have to have some self care, which is also a challenge. How do we have time to take care of our souls and our physical being with so many things to do? It was

---

[4]Rev. Tresa Quarles, minister at St. Stephen's United Church of Christ, Harrisonburg, Virginia.

very hard to take care of myself. I sought out support and counseling from a ministry our conference made available. Another thing that helped a lot was a wonderful ninety-eight-year-old-member who had a wonderful spirit and sense of God's grace. I always felt that God sent her to minister to me! Each time I visited, she would tell me that she didn't know why she was still here, and I would tell her that God still had things for her to teach others. She was truly a guardian angel for me. It really felt as if she were my pastor, though I tried not to tell her my troubles. She simply had a way of reminding me what I was about and somehow managed to refocus my direction by just being herself. It's probably no coincidence that her funeral was one of the last things I did before leaving that church. Her daughter gave me her Bible to use, and I discovered that she had marked and written comments on many passages that held meaning for her. She read it every day of her life. God does indeed provide for our needs.

Once I was in a workshop led by Henri Nouwen, a great theologian. He talked about the importance of taking care of our souls even though it is challenging to find the time to do so. He said even if you have to, put alone time with God on your schedule. Write it on your schedule, and tell your secretary you have an appointment. Do not let anyone disturb you. Who better to make an appointment with than God?

Martin Luther once said you need to spend three hours praying before you start the day. A congregation will be as spiritual as its pastor. Therefore, the pastor must take time for contemplation with God. It is a challenge for women in the ministry, especially if you have family. There is still a societal expectation that women are the primary caregivers in their families, regardless of whatever other responsibilities they have. To be able to do all the pastor must do effectively, you have to take time for self. I learned to combine soul care and physical care together by taking a spiritual walk each morning. It was my prayer time. Spending time talking with

God on a walk was refreshing and good preparation for the day ahead.

It is important that, in caring for our souls, we each have a spiritual friend or a guide. It was difficult for me to find time to do this; but when it became a priority, it was a blessing. I have had the privilege of having three different guides throughout my ministry. Actually, over time, two of them chose no longer to do spiritual direction in the area where I lived. Then, I had to give up meeting my third spiritual director because I moved to a different locality. But I miss having that connection. To meet the challenge of staying close to the heart of God means having someone to walk with you. God speaks through the person and through the exercises in prayer and meditation that we did. My spiritual guides helped me to be a better spiritual guide for my congregational members.

Not only do we need to take care of ourselves spiritually, but we need to take care of our physical selves as well. We get so busy doing God's work that we forget to take care of our bodies. If we want to have many years of ministry in caring for others, we need to care for ourselves. The scripture says, "Love God with all your heart, soul, and mind and your neighbor as yourself" (paraphrased from Mk. 12:30–31). It is not a sin to love yourself enough to take care of yourself spiritually and physically so you can do effective ministry.

My health and my husband's health deteriorated because we did not take time to eat properly. Many times, I did not have time to cook dinner in the evening so I bought fast food. When I had time to cook, I didn't have time to eat slowly because I had a meeting in the evening. I developed a swallowing problem. I was told if I wanted to live, I needed to change my lifestyle when it came to eating. I was to eat slowly, more often, and not a lot at a time.

We are challenged with administrative duties. Rev. Debbie Harmon gives good advice about meeting the challenge of getting everything accomplished. She says:

> Learn to delegate especially that which you don't know how to do. Just today, one of the trustees who

is also chair of the property committee was in fixing a toilet paper holder in the women's bathroom. I would have no idea where to begin a project like that. Know what areas you need someone else to address, then don't be afraid to ask. I am not very computer savvy, and so I asked until one of the members said her son could set up a Web site for the church. Draw on the gifts and talents of others in the church. (Of course, you have to spend time with them and figure out what they are up to!)[5]

A challenge to delegating is that we have to let go and let the other person do the job. They may not do it exactly as we would, but let them do it with guidance and faith. Trust them to use their giftedness in doing the job. I knew I could not do everything in ministry; therefore, I had to delegate. And sometimes I had to hold my breath and my tongue when a delegated item was not done in the manner that I felt it should be done.

At one of my churches, they called me a slave driver because I was after them until something was completed. When delegating, it is best to check back with people to see if they need assistance or just a word of encouragement.

Beautiful things happen in the church when you take the time to ask others to help out. People become more confident and loving, using their talents in the service of God. I have seen members create beautiful items for the church, such as an advent stand and communion table by a gifted carpenter in the church, and I have noticed Bible study leaders develop and grow in their skills and leadership. The minister does not always have to teach the Bible study, but can instead become a participant.

Rev. Wilson finds that property management is one of her least favorite aspects of ministry:

> On my first day at one of my churches a guy knocked on the door—the boiler inspector. I didn't know we

[5]Rev. Debbie Harmon, pastor at the Edinburg Christian Church, Edinburg, Virginia.

had a boiler. I did learn how to bleed boilers. In the interview process at the next church I went to, one of the questions I asked was, 'Do you have a boiler, or do you have forced air?' You end up with just that kind of building maintenance stuff, particularly in small churches. I know it has to be done, but I do not want to explain it. One of the ways the church was trying to save money was they had a cleaning service but no janitor. Well, then when someone called the plumber, either the minister or the secretary had to go and explain what was wrong, which is not my gift. It goes clank, clank, clank, and the water comes out. So that's my least favorite aspect.

I think we meet new challenges in every church to which we are called as pastors. In some situations we follow in the footsteps of women, but certainly not all that frequently. At the four churches I have served, I have followed men who had long pastorates. It was a challenge for all of us in the congregations to get used to one another. Not only was the challenge there for them to get used to a new pastor, but to a woman pastor. I had one secretary who loved being around men, so it was a challenge for her to get used to me. I soon discovered the situation. When one of my male colleagues or any male from the church came in, she was laughing and joking and cutting up. With me, she was much more subdued and "let's get the job done." I had to get used to the fact that some people like to work with the opposite sex better.

As a woman pastor, I have not had a lot of women minister role models. I was the only woman in my Master of Divinity class in seminary and the first woman ordained in my association of the United Church of Christ. Even though the first woman ordained in the United States was Antoinette Brown in 1853 in the Congregational Church, which is now a part of our denomination, we were still slow in accepting women as pastors. I really had not met many women who were in the ministry. I felt the call of God to ministry, and through the encouragement of people in our denomination, I was able to accomplishment this. I felt the challenge to do well as a pastor because I knew I was a role model for other women. I ministered in the ways to which I felt God was calling me. I know that each church I served was truly a call by God.

Going to the church where God is calling you is a challenge. I learned when I started interviewing with churches for a job that I had as much a choice in the matter as did the church. I knew I needed to go where God was calling me. The challenge was not to go where you did not feel God wanted you. I knew I could not take the job because it was a job. It is a calling. It was difficult to say "no" when you did not know when the next opportunity would come for you to say "yes." I found that, with a great deal of prayer and discernment, the calls I accepted were where God wanted me at that time and place.

At one church at which I interviewed, I was picked up in a vacant lot by a church member and taken to a dentist office, where I was interviewed in a conference room. I was never invited to see the church. That was enough for me. I certainly did not feel the call there, and I let them know it with a kind letter.

As I was job seeking, I was privileged to have a choice concerning compensation. Often women are underpaid and have to make a choice of ministry because they need a job. If we are able to bargain and to wait for the right call, it is good. The challenge is for women to know they are paid less than men and to strive to make churches understand ministry is the same for men and women. We all have a job to do. It has cost the same for men and women to go through college and seminary. Both graduate from these owing large sums of money on loans borrowed for their education. Why shouldn't all be paid equally? If a woman is married, the church may feel it does not have to spend money for benefits—the spouse should have to pay for her on his insurance policy. Why should this happen? The church is the one who has hired her to be their minister. They are responsible for taking care of their minister.

Once the minister is in the job, dealing with conflict is a challenge in the church. It is not always conflict between the pastor and the congregation; it is sometimes conflict between parishioners. The pastor has to be very careful as not to take sides or to get in the middle. Many times a pastor is the last to know that a conflict has arisen between parishioners. Sometimes the pastor has to get involved, and should always be available to help, but sometimes the pastor has to be careful not to overstep, or the situation may be made even worse.

Youth leaders were having conflict in one of the churches I served. During the worship service, little notes were being passed around and even across the aisle. After worship, I asked someone what was going on. I learned about the conflict between these two people that was affecting many other people and disrupting worship. I knew something needed to be done and quickly. I asked both parties to meet after church in the fellowship hall. I told them I knew something was going on. They both needed to listen to each other, and each needed to let the other person know how they were feeling and what they saw was the conflict. I became the mediator. They talked and listened. New understanding of each other developed. Everything was fine after that. They worked together and were able to accomplish ministry with the youth.

It worked that time. Another time with different people and at a different church, it did not work. I had to remove myself from the middle of their battle and let them fight it out. This they did by resolving not to get along and going their own ways. There was peace because they no longer yelled at each other. They kept their distance from one another. At one point they both got angry at me. Then I decided they had to settle their own differences. It did not need to be a three-way conflict. Afterward, they were both all right with me but still not with each other. They agreed not to agree. They probably never will, but at least they are not hostile to one another any more.

Rev. Cameron says:

> I think the thing that hurts the most is when I see petty disagreements of the people. That hurts a lot when we talk about love, joy, honor, and privilege of being the church together. The next thing I know

they are fighting over who is going to do what in the kitchen. Some of these disagreements are probably fifty to seventy years old, so I don't know whether I am going to be able to open the door for God to heal those now or not. The most frustrating personal thing I have come against is them not seeming even to want to get along. That's very painful.

The same has been true in marriage counseling. It is a challenge to minister to all parties concerned and remain neutral. You want the best for everyone. It is a challenge not to be judgmental and to help all parties come to a solution that is best for them. Sometimes, the man has thought I was being sentimental to his spouse. Other times it has been the other way around, where the woman feels I am more understanding to the husband. I have been very proud to see couples solve their problems. It is a joy to see them beginning a new life together all over again. It is joy that I have been able to be a part of that. But just as many times, things have not worked out for them. You have to become the one who helps them adjust to the beginning of life apart. Sometimes, I have felt like a failure because I have not been able to help them. Then I see that it has been for the best and that new beginnings are there for them.

These issues are a challenge whether you are a single woman in ministry or married for forty-six years, as I have been. We help who we can, in the ways that they will let us minister to them.

I believe it is a challenge to walk with people through their trials and tribulations and not become overinvolved emotionally. Where children are involved, I have a difficult time not becoming emotionally involved. You have to be strong and have a lot of will power. Being a mother makes it a little more difficult for me to see children hurt. When serving as a pastor in one of our churches, a case in a nearby town involved a child who had been badly abused and murdered. In fact, this was one of several cases, but this was a little girl who had been only two and a half years old. I told the other two pastors in our town—who happened to be men—how I felt. Together we planned a program to lift up our children, show how much we cared, and let them know God loves them. We wanted to challenge the churches and community to respect and protect their children. We held a community service at the fair grounds. About four hundred attended. Each of us three ministers took a part of the sermon that flowed into one message. Our emotions can lead to helping others.

Another time, I was asked to play Mary, the mother of Jesus, as she stood at the foot of the cross where her son was crucified. During this Good Friday service, I was able to put many feelings into the drama because my son was going through some very difficult times in his life. It was not hard for me to play a grieving mother. At the end of my monologue, everyone in the sanctuary was crying. It is all right to become emotionally involved as long as we use it to the good for ourselves and others and draw the appropriate boundaries.

Another challenge you constantly face is to let others know you are a minister. Many people are not used to seeing a female pastor. I have received different reactions when someone learns I am a minister. When going to the hospital to see patients, no questions are asked if I wear a clerical shirt. I am allowed to see the patient immediately.

My clerical shirt creates a lot of conversation. I was walking down the street with my husband in a large city. As we passed a parking lot, the attendant came out to shake my hand. He said he had never seen a woman minister before. We had a conversation about my faith and church as well as about others.

In a restaurant while I was sitting at a table waiting for my husband, a waitress came over and sat down, looked me in the face, and said, "Are you what they call a 'Priestess'?" Again this provided the opportunity to witness to my faith and calling. I have met some very interesting people because of my clerics, and I would not have met them if I had not been wearing them.

I took communion to a parishioner in the nursing home. As we prepared to celebrate the eucharist, her roommate came in. I asked her if she would like communion. Yes, she wanted to participate. As I served her the bread and the cup, she said, "Oh, mother of God." This became my name to her. One of my parishioners was eighty-six years old when I went to the church. She had a hard time remembering I, and not my husband, was the pastor. She knew, but underneath it didn't seem right. She would always introduce me to others as the pastor's wife. Her caregiver would remind her that I was the pastor, and she said, "I know that." She would even call my husband, "Cousin Bob"; but when it came to me, I was still the "pastor's wife."

All of these things call attention to women being ministers. It is good that people realize who you are. The older I have gotten and more known in the church and community, I have chosen not to wear my clerical shirt all the time. I think sometimes I miss the opportunity to do evangelism. Many of the younger women in ministry in our area where we live do not wear the clerics. It does not make us a better minister to wear the clerics, but it does open up the door for conversation and evangelism to witness for Jesus Christ. On the other hand, some people are turned off by the clerics and find it more comfortable to talk with ministers who do not wear them. The challenge is still there to be who we are, regardless of what we wear. Our witness to our faith should come through our words and actions.

As pastors, we especially have a challenge to be genuine and honest. We as women must deal with many things each day. People know if you are genuine or not. Sharing our faith stories helps others as they plan for life. Many women come to me and ask about my faith journey that has led me to being a minister. By sharing my story, others have been led to pursue the ministry.

We must accept the challenge to think outside the box. Judy Blonski is an interfaith minister who has ministered under many and varied circumstances since she was ordained eight years ago. Judy shares:

> Just out of seminary my "call" seemed to lean toward both chaplaincy and pastoral ministry. It was easy to picture myself shepherding my flock on a daily

basis. Complete in robe and stole I visualized tending those in need and those searching for God each in his and her own way. I would imagine generations of the same family standing at the altar to be joined in marriage, their children being baptized, their parents and grandparents being eulogized. It all felt so right. But now, as Paul Harvey says, "Here is the rest of the story."

At first I was able to serve several churches as a "junior pastor." Along about the third year my "call" began changing away from pastoral and I found myself teaching more. This served me well, as my husband's career necessitated moving every few years. It was a blessing in disguise that I was not confined to serving any one church, though from time to time I found myself attending a particular church which would have been such a good "fit" if only I had been able to settle into one place and do as I had always thought I would. However, it seemed God had other plans for me. I wondered during that time if I would ever serve as a traditional pastoral minister.

In retrospect I remember there being much gnashing of teeth and questioning God over my lack of ability to settle in and serve in some definite place and capacity. At some point, however, I began to "look outside the box" of my ego needs, which led to the realization that maybe this was the plan, that I was supposed to travel around the country and use my gifts and talents in a wide variety of ways and share them with many people.

This concept became even clearer as people and situations began "finding" me. I no longer had to seek ways to be my Creator's hands, feet, ears, and eyes. These opportunities to serve just seemed to magically appear. As it is difficult to explain the kind of ministry I have been given, the following is an actual situation from the last eight years.

A friend in Nevada had been holding a yearly Mother's Day tea for the women of her church. For each event she chose a guest speaker, special music, and prepared a menu centered on a particular theme. I was honored to be her second guest speaker and prepared a message of gratitude for everyone there who had ever nurtured someone else, whether or not they had physically given birth. The tea was lovely, and my message well received.

The next day was Mother's Day. I was staying with Anglo friends who lived on a local Nevada Paiute reservation. We had really been looking forward to worshiping together with the tribe in their little United Methodist mission church. During the breakfast we received a call from the minister's wife asking me, "Would you please conduct the service this morning for my husband who is quite ill? No one can be there to play the hymns, either." She did not know I loved to play hymns on the piano! Was I happy to say "yes."

Several times before I had been a guest minister for him in this little church and knew his congregation would be comfortable with this last-minute change. Wearing the only remaining clean clothes I had left, which were quite casual, I glanced at my message of the day before as we headed out the door.

My interfaith training in Native American spiritual rituals stood me in good stead as I created and blessed the Sacred Circle, which encompassed everyone in church that day and the special altar space we were using. After the readings, hymns, and message we all joined hands within a smaller circle. My friend loaned us the use of her "talking feather," which we passed to one another, sharing stories about our mothers or those whom we considered as mothers. Some of the congregants, mostly women with their daughters and grandchildren, spoke in their native languages and translated for our benefit. Many cleansing tears and much joy and gratitude were expressed that morning, even by our lone husband. Once everyone departed the sanctuary, I closed the Sacred Circle and expressed my gratitude to our Creator. Back home with my friends, we talked about how amazingly God works in and through my life. I think it was then I actually began to understand the necessity for all the education and experiences I had ever had. Nothing less would have prepared me so well for the unusual and special times I had already encountered in my short ministry. My soul was lifted in gratitude.[6]

It is a challenge to "look outside the box" and to walk in faith and trust in God. When God calls us, God never leaves or forsakes us. God goes with us and empowered us. Our challenge is to keep learning. It never ends.

Women face unique challenges in ministry. I am sure you can add to the challenges I have listed. Some are unique to each of us; because we are different, we will experience our own individual challenges as women in the ministry. God has created each of us with different personalities and experiences. The way we react to these will vary. No one solution will work every time.

Not all challenges are negative; some are positive. The challenge to use our gift in ministry is very positive. Challenges are good to have because they help us to grow and to see things differently. We can help one another as role models as we share our stories and minister to others.

[6]Rev. Judy Blonski, All Faiths Dialogue and Celebration, San Marcos, California.

5

Ministry Is a Job

After the spiritual journey to ministry, discussing the finer points of theology in seminary, and the joy of graduation and ordination, you might be shocked to find that ministry is indeed a job. Every minister faces such practical concerns as how to get a job, interviews, what to get paid, and determining how your salary package will be distributed. And, as with our female colleagues in other professions, often a disparity exists between our salary and a that of a man doing the same job. A minister endures conversations about hours and benefits, vacation time and personal days. A minister may have special tax forms to fill out. All of this and more comprise the "nitty gritty" of getting hired. Then there are the aspects of doing a job once you get it, filling the many roles expected of a pastor.

For most women in mainline Protestant denominations, the process of getting a ministry position is the same for women as for men. You go through the same channels, jump through the same hoops. First you have to get your degree, usually a Master of Divinity or the equivalent, and then be ordained in your denomination. Then comes the time to look for a ministry position. Often denominational administrators assist you, and they are some of the best advocates for women in ministry. However, you need to know that some local churches simply do not want a woman pastor. This may be especially difficult in congregationally based denominations where the congregational members vote to call a minister. In other denominations with a stronger episcopal structure, the bishop or district superintendent decides where to place ministers. But even then a woman minister might meet resistance.

In his book, *Joined in Discipleship*, Mark G. Toulouse wrote:

> This hesitancy to support women in ministry lasted well into the twentieth century; it still exists in significant pockets of Disciples life today. Janet Riley reveals the interesting autobiographical detail that the Dean of the Disciples House at the University of Chicago, when she applied in 1958, informed her that educational financial assistance there was reserved only for men...Today, women have complete equality in the area of seminary education, but are a long way from being able to claim the same equality in the practice of ministry. Though the Disciples General Assemblies have regularly affirmed, through resolutions, the equality of women in ministry since the 1960s, the general situation in terms of opportunities at the congregational level is only slightly better than it was some twenty years ago. Women, when they can find work in the congregational ministry, generally fill assistant or associate positions. Some are able to assume pastoral ministry in congregations desperate for leadership and unable to pay adequate salaries because men, who have other opportunities, are unwilling to serve in those locations. Regional and general ministry possibilities for women have improved dramatically over the last decade, but only small numbers of these positions are available. The increasing, and tragically underutilized, reservoir of seminary-educated women constitutes the greatest

untapped cumulative resource available to the congregational ministry of the Disciples.[1]

What Toulouse describes is not unique to the Christian Church (Disciples of Christ) by any means. This has been and remains the case in most mainline Protestant denominations. We can be encouraged that the situation is getting better as churches see more and more women in ministry.

Consider one such experience from a congregation in Yorktown, Virginia. This is from a packet of testimonials that is given out by the Virginia Region of the Christian Church (Disciples of Christ) to congregations in the process of calling new pastors, to encourage them to consider calling women pastors. E. Clint Robertson, a Board Chair of Poole Christian Church (Disciples of Christ) wrote, "I am sure that many congregations go in search of a new pastor without giving any thought to maybe, just maybe, considering a woman. Steeped in tradition and conservatism, many congregations will give little or no time to considering a woman to fill their church needs… Being a small conservative congregation I am sure that there were those who had initial misgivings about 'a woman in the pulpit,' but after a few Sundays [of having a woman preaching] those misgivings were proven unfounded."[2]

This packet, called "Women in Ministry in Virginia," is filled with a number of similar stories from congregations who would never think of having a woman as a pastor, and then somehow stumble upon having one (usually initially as an interim minister or as a pulpit supply preacher), and find out that (what do you know!) she isn't so bad after all! While it is good for congregations to hear this and know this, and it is good that denominational staff encourage congregations in hiring women, it is discouraging to think there even needs to be such a packet of testimonials. The fact that some congregations still need to be told that women can be

---

[1]Mark G. Toulouse, *Joined in Discipleship* (St. Louis: Chalice Press, 1992), 155–56.

[2]"Women in Ministry in Virginia," compiled by the Christian Church in Virginia.

ministers is discouraging, to say the least. But the good news is that your denominational leaders stand at the forefront of the struggle and are often your best advocates. I know some of the regional ministers in charge of the search and call process in my denomination will not separate out the files of female candidates, even when a search committee tells them they will not consider a woman minister. They send them, saying it is their job to send the papers of the most qualified candidates. They even spend extra time trying to educate and encourage such search committees to consider women ministers. So get to know those in your denomination who are responsible for "search and call"/placement of ministers, and let them get to know you. They will be your best allies in finding a position, often your best advocates in the field, and can match you with the best congregations for you.

In the area where I (Debra) served in my first position was a smaller congregation with about one hundred members and a Sunday worship attendance of around fifty. They had apparently (begrudgingly) accepted a woman pastor in the 1980s, and were so impressed by her ministry that they consistently called women as their pastors after that. In fact, they had a male pastor when I first began, and he seemed to experience some resistance and resentment that he attributed to the fact that he wasn't a woman!

When I arrived at my first fulltime position after seminary and ordination, I was the only female at our area Disciples ministers meetings. Within a couple of years, another church in our area hired a woman as solo pastor. Now I hear that there are at least four or five women at the area ministers meetings, and a couple of them are senior ministers at multi-staff churches. Likewise, when I got to my current position two and a half years ago, I was the only female minister out of thirteen churches in the area (and the first my church had ever had). Now, there are women pastors at three out of the thirteen churches, and I have heard a number of times, "Oh, you're that new lady pastor at the Christian church. I've heard a lot of good things about you." To hear such comments is very gratifying to this "lady pastor."

Women in ministry need to utilize the available resources in finding a call—denominational staff and printed materials, testimonials from other churches that have had and enjoyed a woman in the pulpit, the recommendations of others—to open doors that might have been previously closed. Once a congregation has experienced a woman in the ministry, one hopes they will come around to seeing what a good thing it is! And sometimes we have to be our own ambassadors and fulfill our callings in such a way that the door will be opened for the sisters who come after us.

As you are looking for a church or ministry position, you of course need to ask yourself questions that apply to anyone searching for a job, such as where do I want to live? What area of the country do I prefer? Do I like big cities, or quiet, country towns? Would I prefer to live on one of the coasts, in the Midwest, or in the South? Do I want to be close to my family, or am I willing to be farther away? What kind of position do I want? Do I want the freedom of being a solo pastor, or the support and connection an associate pastor at a multi-staffed church would find? What sort of salary package am I aiming for?

These will not all be in your control to determine, but it helps if you think about these things as you are choosing where you will go. Think about yourself and where you will work best. Would you be bored to tears in a rural area, or enjoy the easy, laid-back pace? Can you live a few states away from your family and friends, or do you need to be closer, for whatever reason? Often in the ministry, you go where the job is; however, you can set parameters. Ultimately, it is up to you and God's leading whether or not you accept a particular position.

I have a friendly suggestion, though: do not be too confined by your expectations. You never know what awaits you if you are willing to expand your horizons. Case in point: the most recent time I was in the search and call process, in filling out my papers for the denomination I asked to stay in Indiana or a neighboring state. I had put down that I would like to be a co-pastor or associate pastor at a multi-staffed church, mainly because that was what I was used to. I also put I wanted to be in a metropolitan or suburban area, again because that is what I was used to. Imagine my surprise when I got a call from a little church in Virginia, in a town that I had trouble finding on a map.

At first it was just polite conversation, because it had never crossed my mind to move so far from my family. As the interviews progressed, we seemed a good fit, and so I agreed to visit and do a trial sermon. At that point I figured it would just be a nice long weekend in Virginia, to a place I had never been, and that would be the end of it. As we were talking, the chair of the search committee told me he had looked at my papers and put them aside a number of times, because, by the preferences I had indicated, we didn't seem to be a good match. But we were a good match, and to my surprise, they extended a call. I accepted, and now I live in Virginia. It has been a wonderful call, and we have done some exciting ministry together. In my spare time I have gotten to know another part of the country. So be willing to step outside what is comfortable and familiar to you. Know what you want, and what is nonnegotiable, but also allow that the Spirit can move you to amazing places if you are willing to go.

Another thing, girls—you might have to negotiate your own contract. If your denomination does not have a set contract or package (usually based on church size and giving), then you are basically a free agent. If so, you need to do your research, go in knowing what you want, what is reasonable to expect from a congregation of that size, and don't let your own insecurities handicap you. Now is not the time to be a shrinking violet. In the April 2006 issue of *Money* magazine, the central article was a comparison of married men and women and how they deal with money. Interestingly, they found that while women handle more of the day-to-day finances for couples (paying bills, budgeting, day-to-day spending), the men were still responsible for the larger financial decisions. In their survey, they found that 73 percent of men, as opposed to 22 percent of women, claimed to be responsible for investment decisions; 66 percent of men were responsible for retirement planning, as opposed to 25 percent of women; and 60 percent of men were responsible for insurance decisions, as opposed to 34 percent of women. Furthermore, only 45 percent of men thought saving for retirement was important to their wives, while in fact, 68 percent of women said saving for retirement was very important.[3]

The point is, while we women have come a long way in assuming financial responsibility and independence, some stereotypes still exist. We sometimes buy into them. While we balance the checkbook at home, we also need to educate ourselves about our larger financial picture and become comfortable in talking about it. We might feel it "unfeminine" or "impolite" to discuss money matters openly, or we might simply not have had experience doing so, and so feel unsure and insecure. We need to overcome those obstacles if we are going to succeed in ministry or any other profession.

Men might make inaccurate assumptions about what we know and value financially. As the article in *Money* suggested, women need to step up and assume responsibility for their own finances. Do not allow your lack of confidence to cause you to abdicate your responsibility or go into salary negotiations with weak knees. Educate yourself. Know your financial situation. Know that even though they are Christians, some church members will not pay any more for a minister than they absolutely have to. Some will try to strong-arm you, just because that is the way they are used to doing business. If they know they can take advantage of you at the outset of your ministry, it does not bode well for the future of your ministry. While they are your brothers and sisters in Christ, they are also potentially going to be your parishioners. They should be respected as such, but you also need to respect yourself and give them reason to respect you. If they see you can respect yourself, they are more likely to respect you and your ministry as well.

As a friendly suggestion, we as women need to be aware of any tendency we have to yield on money issues.

---

[3]Pat Regnier and Amanda Gengler "Men, Women and Money," *Money,* vol. 35, no. 4 (April 2006): 92–94, 98.

In negotiations, be polite and considerate, but also be frank. Know what ministers in your denomination make at equivalent churches. Know standards for time off, parsonage, professional expenses, and so on. While there are standards in some denominations, some require ministers to "work out their own salvation," pardon the pun. To go into salary negotiations fully prepared, you may have to do some research on health insurance, pension plans or IRAs, or other benefits.

Also remember that some smaller churches are limited in what they can pay a minister, so think about how much you are willing to compromise. Smaller churches sometimes compensate a smaller salary by offering a parsonage, or free yard care, or homegrown vegetables in the summer. Again, think about what you are willing to accept, and don't go into a position feeling slighted or misused, because those feelings will impact your ministry.

In one of my contract negotiations, I had a member of the search committee who proposed seven days of vacation. At first I was pleasantly surprised, thinking he meant seven Sundays of vacation (which is how churches sometimes count vacation time), along with the accompanying weeks. What he meant was one week off per year. Knowing that the average in my denomination, as well as most others, is 4 weeks per year (not counting educational and conference time), I could not accept one week. I knew that I would be cheating myself and was able to show the committee, using research I had done, that four weeks was standard. And so I have four weeks of vacation.

Others have had to negotiate for vacation time and personal time. A friend who is a new grandmother told her church that she is not going six months without seeing her grandchild. She does not want her grandchildren growing up without knowing her, and she wants to know them as well. So she has been negotiating with her church for "grandma visits" every two to three months, and says they have been very understanding, as many of them are grandparents as well.

One of the ways I persuaded my search and call committee to give me four weeks of vacation a year was telling them one of the weeks would be spent visiting family back in Indiana. Churches and committees can be very understanding when it comes to family ties and obligations. This is my first church outside of my home state, and I have never lived more than two hours from my family. We try to see each other every three to four months at least, because I want to be a part of their lives, and vice versa. Church members usually understand and appreciate a minister's family connections. And the care and concern they show in contract negotiations is sometimes a good indicator of how they will care for you as their minister.

However, I also know that churches will not give any more than they have to. At my first church out of seminary, my package included $25,000 in salary and two weeks of vacation. In later years I negotiated more vacation time when they could not afford a salary increase, but I still finished seven years later at under $30,000 and with three weeks of vacation a year. This can be attributed to my ignorance or being naïve, but the fact is I lost thousands of dollars.

Now you might be saying ministry isn't about money. How can we be concerned with material wealth when we should be more concerned with spiritual riches? We should not be so greedy or hard-nosed. No, we should not. But if we do not value ourselves, our ministry, and our training, how can we expect those we serve to respect them?

You also might meet some resistance or resentment around vacation, conference, or educational time. Again, you need to be able to calmly, but firmly, explain why such time is necessary. We ministers invest a lot of ourselves in what we do, and we need time to take a break, to recharge our batteries, to have some balance. We may need to explain why we need time off, not in a defensive way, but for our own well-being. Of course, we have a good biblical and theological model in the concept of the Sabbath that we can use in our explanations. But many times on a search committee or pastoral relations committee, you will be working with folks who themselves get maybe two weeks of vacation a year (and perhaps do not take those). They may work 50–60 hours or more a week, and expect you to as well. You need to learn about clergy self-care, to know what your limits and needs are, and bring those to the table for honest negotiations.

You also need to have some basic understanding of your tax situation. Ministry is notorious for its complicated tax scheme. Between self-employment taxes and social security offset, housing allowances and parsonages, expense accounts and mileage, it can all seem overwhelming. It doesn't have to be. Remember the papers you wrote and the books you read to get through seminary and become ordained? Do you realize how much intelligence and stamina you must have at your disposal to have gotten to where you are? Well, now you have to take that same determination and do your homework again. Understand your financial situation. Set up your salary package so it will be to your best advantage at tax time. Know what is needed, and also be ready to show an under-informed, volunteer church treasurer what is needed. Many church treasurers are even more clueless than you when it comes to your financial situation and needs.

Another challenge women in ministry face is progressing up the career ladder within the church. A 1998 National Congregations Survey by the Alban Institute (www.alban.org/NatCongStudy.asp), with 1236 congregations participating, looked at the gender of the head or senior clergy in those congregations: 1026, or 83 percent, were male; 114, or 9.2 percent, were female. (In 96, or 7.7 percent, of the congregations they were between permanent pastors.) So men had the clear majority in positions of senior leadership. Some churches will be willing to hire women as associate or co-pastors, but we are not as well represented in solo or senior pastor positions. Hopefully with time this will change. In the meantime, realize that it might be more difficult for you to advance in your career than it is for your male colleagues. But it is your career, and you must take responsibility for it. In a department meeting while working in a temp job when I was in the search and call process for a year and a half, the manager was telling of positions that were opening up, some of which required advanced training. She said something to the effect, "While this may mean some extra work on your part, remember, this is your career. No one else is going to do it for you." Likewise, in your ministry career, we all need to decide where we want to go, what we want to do, and how much we are worth when we get there.

In thinking about career advancement, we also need to take into account denominational administrative positions. Think about your own interests, gifts, and talents and where they can best be used in ministry. To paraphrase the apostle Paul, some of us are administrators, some teachers, some advocates, and some pastors. I know women in my denomination who are regional ministers, lead volunteers in mission, are seminary professors, or pastors in local congregations. There is room for all of our gifts and ministries—find yours and use them. When you begin doing ministry, you might be surprised what aspects of ministry you really enjoy. In doing youth ministry, I found a passion for mission work and outreach ministries I did not fully realize I had in seminary. While I always thought I couldn't preach every week because I didn't have enough to say, I find I love the teaching aspects of preaching and am rather enjoying it as a weekly discipline. So know your talents and interests, but also allow yourself to grow and develop those gifts you do not yet know you have.

Also note that as you work with other churches at the local minister's association, or just as you go about doing your job, you might encounter members of other, more conservative, denominations who do not appreciate or even recognize women as ministers. According to Wikipedia.com, as cited in *DisciplesWorld*, there are one billion Catholics worldwide, and they do not ordain women; there are 105 million classified as Pentecostals (although estimates vary widely), and many of them do not ordain women.[4] Even in our mainline Protestant denominations, as we have seen, many members do not approve of women in ministry. So within the body of Christ you are likely to meet some opposition to your ministry.

---

[4]"By the Numbers," cited in *DisciplesWorld*, vol. 5, no. 4 (May 2006): 4, from www.wikepedia.com.

These are situations you will have to handle according to your own conscience, and hopefully with a measure of grace. They can vary from something said in jest, to a diatribe about why there should be no women in ministry. As mentioned earlier, a clergywoman friend in Indiana went to the local ecumenical gathering of clergy, and found herself sitting at a table with all men. As they went around introducing themselves, she said she was the pastor of the local Christian Church. Someone said, "Isn't it nice that the little woman is a pastor?" She felt decidedly dismissed at that point, and was then excluded from the table conversation. True, this was in a town known for being conservative, but it happens in other places, too. If there is anywhere you might experience discrimination or be dismissed as a woman in ministry, it may very well be in ecumenical circles, at local ministers' meetings, and in relating to other denominations.

Most of the time, in most situations, we can just agree to disagree, and be about the business at hand. If another chooses to press the issue, then respond as you choose. Be secure in your own call to the ministry, and be able to explain logically and reasonably your understanding of your call as a woman to the ministry. Try not to be defensive. And don't try to "out argue" someone who is trying to convince you. As Rev. Geneal Wilson noted:

> I do find discrimination, less now than when I first started, but it's still there in ecumenical settings, in community settings... It's a little less pronounced than it was twenty years ago, but it's still there.[5]

In the best of situations, these conversations occur in a context of Christian charity and grace. If not, you may be challenged to be the more grace-full person in the conversation, and simply accept that they disapprove. If they are hostile, aggressive, or abusive, then by all means, walk away and avoid them in the future. We also may need to educate and equip the members of our churches for occasions when they

---

[5]Rev. Geneal Wilson, pastor at Strasburg Christian Church, Strasburg, Virginia.

are confronted by others who challenge them about having a woman minister. Offering them some scriptures they can use that provide authority or support for women in ministry is an option. It is not always just our personal sense of calling, but sometimes it is an issue of pastoral care of our members, and we need to support and encourage them for when they are faced with this challenge.

Sometimes we need to step up to the plate and assert our presence in ecumenical or community gatherings. Rev. Susie Cameron offers this encouraging example:

> I had a hard time getting my foot in the door of the ministerial association in Anderson. I've been going to some of the meetings a year or so, and I did participate in the Good Friday service a year ago. This year we haven't been meeting as often. I went to the Good Friday service, and all of the men filed in and sat in their chairs… I got on their case afterwards. I said there were not any women ministers on that platform. I said if this is the clergy association of Anderson, these days there are lots of us [women]. So I'm now on the executive board. I have my foot in the door. I think that's a step.[6]

If we see something that needs to be changed, sometimes we need to be the agent of change that makes it happen. If you can, find helpful constructive ways to bring about change in your area, so that others who perhaps do not have the chance in their own denomination can see a woman in ministry.

In addition to such issues as finding a call, negotiating a salary package, and working within the religious community, each woman finds she has some gifts and talents that are particularly suited to the job of ministry. One pastoral role I have found that I just love is that of administrator. I am quite well suited by talent and temperament for the organizational aspect of ministry. As a pastor, you are at times

---

[6]Rev. Susie Cameron, pastor at East Lynn Christian Church, Anderson, Indiana.

a manager, a director. Some of us are natural administrators. However, it is sometimes hard for women to be managers or directors, especially if they feel they are not accustomed to administration. Yet as a woman, you often have to manage the household budget, balance the checkbook, organize schedules, monitor diets and food intake, plan meals and shop for groceries, and so on and so on. Don't these tasks require some management skill? Don't we, as women, have wonderful skills as domestic administrators? Can't we then apply some of these skills to our work in the "household of faith"? I think we can.

As a pastor you may be (read "will be") challenged at a meeting or about a pet project. As women we might take it personally or get our feelings hurt. We might not be used to playing "hardball" as some are accustomed to in corporate boardrooms. We have been trained to be pastoral and compassionate, but we have not always been trained well to handle administrative challenges. While it is always good to be passionate about your ministry, it sometimes helps to take a more balanced view to get the job done. We have to plan and program, but we also have to realize there will be conflicts that must be resolved.

Another part of the job that I think women have natural inclinations for is as coordinators of church programming. We are used to multi-tasking, to juggling a number of things at once, and in a church this becomes very helpful. In one day, you may be writing a sermon, meeting with a family to plan a funeral, planning the monthly newsletter, and attending a finance committee meeting. Many areas of ministry call for coordination: worship, education, membership, evangelism, outreach, mission, stewardship, property, and finance. For all that we do—preaching, teaching, counseling, administering, and coordinating the various ministries of the church—we have to be able to do them all at once. We need to keep a number of "balls in the air," and also keep the various ministries connected and communicating.

Probably the most key ingredient to successful ministry I have found is communication. We women are natural communicators. (We have been shown to be more verbal from the cradle!) We as pastors need to communicate with our members, between ministries in the church, and with the outside community. This requires constant vigilance, but reaps a great reward. Use bulletins, newsletters, cards, Web sites, banners, and bulletin boards to keep your congregation up to date and informed. Use local newspapers, radio, street signs, and even TV ads to communicate what you are doing to the larger community. Remember, even the greatest ministry idea is worthless if no one knows about it. When it comes to your church and ministry, talk it up!

Another talent that helps us in coordinating the work of the church is identifying and recruiting members for various tasks. We as women are used to enlisting people to do jobs ("Pick up your room"; "Honey, you need to mow the yard"; "Clean the animal's cage"; etc.), so I think it comes quite naturally to us to recruit people for tasks at the church, and then to check with them to make sure they are following through in doing their jobs. This also gets more people involved in the ministry of the church, gives them a greater sense of ownership, and helps them respect the concept of the ministry of all believers.

Finally, along with being coordinators and recruiters, I think we women are good cheerleaders. Not all of us were the cheerleader type in school (I certainly wasn't!), but we encourage others. My husband (who is also an ordained minister) is fond of reminding me that the name Barnabas (Paul's friend on his missionary journeys) means "son of encouragement." He was one who encouraged others. We women are often "daughters of encouragement," cheering others on, telling them when they do a good job, noticing when something goes right. That is a talent and gift that serves us well in ministry and is greatly appreciated.

Hopefully this chapter has given you the chance to think about aspects of ministry as a job, such as finding a ministry position, negotiating a contract, advancing up the career ladder, dealing with discrimination, and using the talents and abilities we women have that help us to do our ministries. We are administrators, teachers, cheerleaders, communicators, recruiters, counselors, advisors, mediators, advocates, and encouragers. We are gifted for all of these tasks. While ministry is sometimes a challenging job, the women I have talked to agree that it is a joy, and they cannot imagine doing anything else.

6

Being a Minister and a Woman Too

Being a woman in the ministry is a blessing and a challenge. The greatest blessing is being able to live out your calling to ministry and to be whom you are: a woman created in the image of God. The challenges that can also be blessings come to us regardless of age or status of marriage. In fact, all ministers, regardless of gender, have challenges to face. A colleague told me that his challenge was being too young, while mine was being a woman in ministry.

Challenges are different due partly to expectations that vary between women and men. Certainly male and female ministers both have challenges, but expectations and responsibilities are different. God calls us to ministry, and all of our roles are important.

Women do not fit the perfect description of a minister who is a twenty-five-year-old man with the experience and knowledge of someone who has been in the ministry for forty years. There are always expectations of the minister, regardless of whether you are a man or a woman. We also have expectations of ourselves. Sometimes these are the hardest to deal with. How can you be a minister, wife, mother, sister, daughter, *and* friend? After becoming a minister when you are already a wife and mother, how do you live up to all the expectations everyone has for you and you have for yourself? Or, it can be the other way around: How do you deal with being a minister and then having a family? How do you balance everything? How do you minister as a single woman or as a single mother?

I (Barbara) went into the ministry later in life. At forty-two years of age, married with two children, I left a job I had for eleven years in the public school system. I went back to college and seminary.

When I started back at college, every member of our family endured many changes. I was also serving a small church as a student pastor. When you choose to respond to God's call, it is your call; however, it also affects other people. Your family and friends may not understand this. Their expectations are that you will remain the same and be able to do all of the same things you used to do. Some of my family and friends did not understand my new role as a student and a minister.

When my family decided to have a reunion, I already had a wedding scheduled. Some of my family could not understand why I could not get a substitute for the wedding. My husband and children traveled 256 miles to the reunion without me. They understood why I could not go with them.

As you are changing, so do the situations and the people around you. I used to look into the mirror and say, "Where has Barbara gone?" I didn't even know who I was or who I was becoming. I knew I was different. I was studying and serving a church. I did not have the time to go places and do things that I used to do. I lost some friends because we no longer had the same things in common. But God has a way of blessing us with new friends, new aspirations, and new goals. I liked who I was becoming.

The ministry brings so many unexpected joys. You begin to appreciate them. A meeting or a class is cancelled, and you get to spend an evening at home. What a blessing!

In our role as minister and woman, we have to deal with guilt. Sometimes, we expect ourselves to be everything to all people, and it is impossible. When we do not reach our own expectations, we feel guilty. When something does not go smoothly, then it is our fault. When we realize we are not God and we cannot do it all, we have peace within and get more done. With God's help, "all things are possible."

Balance is needed in our lives. This comes with setting priorities. Yes, our job needs to be first, or does it? What about family? Priorities change. Flexibility is a must. How do you turn off being a minister and return to being a wife and mother? You are all of these, but sometimes one needs to be mother and not be minister. This has been really difficult for me. I have been an ordained minister for seventeen years. Most of the time, ministry came first because my children were grown and had families of their own. My husband was retired and loved to do his own thing. However, even though my family was not demanding of me, sometimes I had to place them first.

A friend, Mary Lou, who is an interim in California, shared with me that her mother still worries that she will ruin her marriage when she takes an interim where she needs to live away from home part of the week. Even though her mother knows Mary Lou's husband of forty years supports her, her mother still feels Mary Lou is not fulfilling the "traditional" role of a wife and might be the cause of breaking up her marriage.

Another friend, Janice, said one of her sisters struggles with Janice's ministry, because she is insecure about her own life choices and often takes Janice on because of her position on some social issues. Their relationship is often difficult, even though Janice has really tried hard enough not to talk about her "religion" when the family is together. Not one of Janice's family members have ever heard her preach, nor ever expressed any desire to. Though distance is somewhat a factor, they did at least attend her ordination.

Balancing roles in families is difficult. Ann Graves says:

> I am blessed that my husband has always been extremely supportive. Since we do not have children,

I have been able to do things that many cannot. The biggest challenge has been living apart during some of my interims. Since the distances were large enough, I needed to stay in the community where I was serving the church. However, I've never gone so far that I could not return home at least one day each week, and my husband visits whenever he is able. We make it work. There's also the plus in these situations that when I am home, I am truly absent from the church.[1]

Geneal Wilson talks about balancing roles in her life:

I'm sixty-two years old, so that's kind of the break...or time between the Baby Boomers and the traditionalists. I think our marriage started out very traditional, although not rigidly so. My mother was very liberated, early. But there are just things you automatically fall into. Ministry was a second career for me, so there was some working through. "We're now working on my schedule, not your schedule." Had my husband still been working, that would have been another issue. It bothers me, I mean, at times I would like to be free on the weekends. So that's something everyone faces, whether you are male or female. It is a balancing of roles.

I chose very intentionally, for my son's wedding, not to participate as officiant. I just wanted to be a mom. So I have made those kinds of decisions. In a way I think I've found it easier than many women, simply because I came to this at the point where my children were pretty well independent. By the time I graduated and was ordained, both boys were in college and out of the house. So it wasn't like I had small children at home. I would think that would have been a very difficult thing and would have made balancing those roles more difficult. I had enough

---

[1]Rev. Ann Graves, interim pastor, State College, Pennsylvania.

trouble when the grandkids came, that I couldn't go and be there. I don't think it's a whole lot different for men and women, particularly with younger men who are being so much more active in the raising of their children and that sort of thing.

Concerning the care of parents, had I not been the minister, my guess is I would have gone with Pete to care for his mother when she had health issues. As it was, I couldn't go; and I couldn't get him to go and deal with it. These are just those family dynamic kinds of things.

When we were working out the call to my last church, I said, "I will take vacation the first year because there is no way I will not be able to go see grandkids.'" It was a non-issue really for the congregation. I think you need to be real clear about that.

The friend thing is an issue. I think girlfriends tend to share more than guy friends share. Every place I have been, there have been women who want to be my best friend. To not turn them off, but to be able to keep the distance that I feel is necessary as their pastor has been a difficult balancing act. I would say that might be the most difficult balancing act.[2]

Susie Cameron shares her experiences in balancing roles in her life as a woman minister:

Tom is just so supportive and has been from the beginning, so there are no real problems. On a normal day, church is my life, and he's fine with that. Saturday morning is our time. We go out for breakfast, and then we do our chores. That's our time together that's sacred. I've never had a problem with him.

Now the grandmother thing is a problem, because I would love to be in Florida. Within the last two weeks, a minister in Florida resigned. Within two days they were on the phone to me and wanted me.

---

[2]Rev. Geneal Wilson, pastor at Strasburg Christian Church, Strasburg, Virginia.

The hardest thing I've ever done is say I can't consider it, because he left them in the middle of a building project. I said I will not do to my congregation what he has done to you. I have made a long-term commitment to where I am at this time, and I intend to honor that. The only thing that would keep me from doing that is that if I feel my work is done, or if they don't want me anymore.

Now my grandchildren are in Florida, and I'm in Indiana, so how have I handled it? I have told my congregation that I am not going six months without seeing them. I am going to see them every three months or so. I have been negotiating this year so I can go every two or three months to see them. The congregation has been very understanding. I will not let our grandchildren grow up and not know me. And I don't want to not know them. I think we are going to work it out OK. But it's very painful. It is such a joy. You know, I have days when I want to run away from it. But I have no question God called me to that place and that my work there is not done. And it's a joy to be a part of that.[3]

Helen is a young mother of two who was divorced for several years. She remarried at the end of the first year of a new pastorate. Here she was a minister, a mother, and a newlywed in a new church. Helen says it is a challenge to balance all of these roles. The congregation is very understanding. Her husband, who is also a minister in a different denomination than hers, is very supportive and understanding. She is conscientious and organized in her ministry. She is very energetic. She manages to do her ministry and care for her children and husband successfully. She has worked it out with the church to take a three-week vacation with her family every summer. When the children are ill, she stays home with

---

[3]Rev. Susie Cameron, pastor at East Lynn Christian Church, Anderson, Indiana.

them. When she is called to visit someone in the hospital at 6:30 in the morning, she is there. She says with the support of her husband, she is able to accomplish the many facets of her role as a minister and a woman with a family.

I have had the good fortune of being able to do ministry close to our children and grandchildren for the last nine years. Before this we lived about 256 miles away, where I served a church. I am so glad that I was able to receive a call to a church close to family. I truly appreciated the fact I lived close to my family when a tragedy occurred, although I found it very difficult to separate my roles. It was difficult to know which role I needed to be in.

On a Friday morning, May 13, 2005, we received a call that our sixteen-year-old grandson and our son-in-law were in a plane crash. The accident happened about ten miles from our home. They were taken to a hospital an hour and a half from where we lived. We met our son and his wife who had gone to the school to pick up our granddaughter, whose father and brother were in the crash. We traveled to the hospital together where we met our daughter. Partly being in shock and partly due to the minister coming out in me, it was very difficult to go from minister to mom and grandmother. I was with my daughter and our grandson when he died. I comforted her. Her heart was broken in two. I think mine was also. I had prayer with my son-in-law, who was fighting for his life. I thought, "This can't be happening to our family. Things like this happen to everyone else's family, but not ours." Our grandson, Daniel, died at 5:30 p.m., about six hours after the plane crash. All night we were in a prayer vigil for our son-in-law, Richard. He died the next morning at 8:30.

All during this time we had a room full of ministers and friends from my daughter's church. She and her husband and children were involved in two churches. Our son-in-law was ordained in prison ministry. He also did a plane ministry. At spring break from the university where he worked, he went to Florida and flew a plane carrying religious banners along the coast of Miami. He was an excellent pilot.

On the day of the accident, Richard and Daniel were flying in a 1942 aircraft. They were doing what they liked to do best. They had a very close father-and-son relationship.

At the hospital, our daughter's ministers and friends comforted her. I had to accept a different kind of ministry from what I was used to doing. Coming from my background and from my counseling experiences, I was used to giving families time to grieve together without hovering over them. Maybe it was because there were so many of them around—seven ministers and a room full of friends. In fact, the hospital chaplain found us a room just for our family and friends to be in. It was a blessing for some and others not so much a blessing. We all grieve differently.

The plane crash happened the day before Pentecost. We were having communion in both churches I serve and confirmation in one. I went to church and conducted communion and the confirmation of two young men whom I had been teaching for months. From the time I received a call about the crash, I was in touch with both churches through one of our secretaries, whom I asked to call and let everyone know in both churches. I have wonderful trained leaders who are excellent speakers. I had the secretary ask one of these to deliver the sermon, but I did the rest of the services.

The day after the memorial service for our family members, I conducted a funeral for a church member. The day before the memorial service, I visited in the home of the member who died. I stopped and picked up breakfast and took it to the surviving family member, and we made funeral arrangements. It was faith in God that kept me going. This was truly one of those times when God was carrying me.

During those services that I conducted, I felt very close to God and to my loved ones who had died. I could feel Daniel's spirit hovering in the church that Sunday morning. I have never felt closer to God than at those moments. God's strength and refuge gave me the power to minister that day. I had baptized my grandson. As I stood before the two young men being confirmed that day, I could also see Daniel there. But truly the presence of his spirit was with me. The congregational members were wonderful. I did not talk to many people, and some just held me. They were my ministers that day, in addition to my associate conference minister, who came to sit in the congregation with my husband. He was there to support me if I needed him to take over the service. I needed God's strength that day, as well as the love and compassion of my congregation.

At times we must let our congregation minister to us. The call to ministry is a covenantal relationship in which pastor and people care for each other. As pastor I promised "to serve the church faithfully, preaching and teaching the word of God, administrating the sacraments, and fulfilling the pastoral office according to the faith and order of the United Church of Christ." The congregation promised "to labor with me in the ministry of the gospel and to give due honor and support as we gathered in mutual ministry."[4]) The congregations grieved with me as we found strength together.

At first, the minister kept coming out in me. I was strong for everyone. Finally, two weeks later, I broke down and cried. My grieving process began. It was a challenge to be grieving myself while helping others grieve at the same time. My roles kept getting mixed up. I was torn between them. But God was good to me, because after the funeral of a member in the church a few days after our memorial service, I did not have a funeral for seven months. That has never happened in ministry for me. I have always had many funerals close together.

Everything changed in our lives. Ministry always came first, but with this tragedy our family has come to mean so much to each one of us and to the way I do ministry. Some things are trivial, such as making a mistake in the bulletin. Who cares as long as it doesn't say something terribly wrong? Perhaps someone hasn't given you an article for the newsletter. They missed the deadline. If it is not in this month's newsletter, it can be in the next month's.

---

[4]From *Book of Worship of the United Church of Christ* (New York: United Church of Christ Office for Church Life and Leadership, 1986).

I never allowed time for family before, but now I make sure I have time for them. Balancing time in ministry and fulfilling our many roles takes planning. Sometimes our personal families need us as much as our church families. With God's help and lots of prayer, we can keep track as to what God wants us to do in keeping balance between ministry, family, and friends.

Part of ministry is to equip the saints of the church to be ministers using their gifts and talents. I have been fortunate in the four churches that I have served as student pastor and pastor to have people who are very willing to help in all situations. When I went into the ministry, someone gave me some sound advice: "Love God, love people, and love yourself." Sounds like Jesus giving the greatest commandments to his disciples. I remember telling my first church as an ordained minister, that I was not there to please 382 different members but to please one and that was God. As a minister, I did not have the time to get into people's little games. We were there to spread the good news of Christ in words and actions.

We must keep balance in our ministry, family, and friends. If we concentrate fully on only one of these, the others will suffer. Many times it has felt as if I have all these plates twirling on sticks. I get one going. Then I go to another, and then I start another one and another. About the time I get all my plates twirling, it is time to go back to the beginning. To keep balance is to take time for God, for people, and for yourself. It is difficult to keep all going at the same time, but possible with God.

To keep balance in our lives is to take time with God to study, meditate, pray, and spend time in fellowship with other colleagues. This helps to put everything into perspective. A lot of times God speaks to me through dreams and visions. It is good to pay attention. I remember a very challenging funeral I had to conduct. I had prayed a lot. As I stood at the pulpit, I saw an angel standing in the doorway at the back of the church. I was stunned but felt peace. I even looked twice to see if it was the sun shining a certain way. I could not believe my eyes. But no, the figure was there for a moment and then disappeared. God has a way of bringing you these awe-inspiring moments when you need them the most.

Another time, I had a dream about our son John, whom we had left behind in Virginia. He was living in our previous home by himself. When we moved to Pennsylvania, we moved out. Usually the children move out of the family home, but not with us. I was very worried about our son. I had the most disturbing dream. I saw John and a dove flying toward him. I thought, "Oh, no. He is going to die." The next day, I was traveling to Virginia for Thanksgiving with the family. I dwelt on it all the way down the road during two and one-half hours in Pennsylvania, the half hour through Maryland, and then, finally, driving through West Virginia, I knew what my dream meant. John was going to be all right. The dove was a symbol sent from God that God would take care of John and he would be safe. When I first saw John after arriving, he said, "Mom, I have something to tell you. I had this dream that a man was standing beside me with his hand on my shoulder. It was Jesus." God had sent us both a message. What peace and security we both felt when I told him my dream. If we give God a chance, God shows us revelations that sustain us for balance in ministry.

I have also found new, exciting ways to help others. I wanted to go to an Easter play at another church, but did not want to go alone. I called one of my parishioners. It brought new life to her. Treating her as a person of worth made her feel like she was special. It opened up doors for her to become active in the church and brought to me a lasting friendship.

To keep balance is to think about others, but also to know your limitations. As you think about others and give of yourself to them, you are blessed in return. At one of our teacher's workshops many years ago, the speaker said, "Give 100 percent of yourself to whatever you are doing. If you only have 85 percent to give, then give 100 percent of the 85 percent you have to give." When you are ministering at the church, give it your all. When you are with family, they desire and deserve your undivided attention.

Sometimes that is difficult because you may have a church member who is very ill. But for the few minutes that you can be with your family, truly be with them in mind, body, and spirit. Taking time for family is important because it builds relationships. Family members need family members to depend on. All relationships take time. When in the church, work on relationships with people. When with family, work on relationships with them. With God's help, lessons learned in each will carry over into the other. Family relationships can be difficult when you are in the ministry, because you are on call twenty-four hours a day for emergencies. People in the congregation need you to be with them in their crises because you are a part of their spiritual family; you help them in their connection to God. They see the compassionate caring Christ in you. To balance your ministry and family is difficult, but with God's help you can do it by loving God and others.

A healthy focus on others, rather than on ourselves and on the demands we feel, can help us find balance. Visitation has always been a major part of my ministry. This helps to build relationships. In seminary, when I needed a break from studying, I would visit members from the church where I was serving as a student pastor. The break away from studying helped to bring new focus. I went back to studying with new energy and a new outlook.

I know that our family situation is different from others. When going back to school at forty-two years of age, it was difficult balancing everything that was going on in my life. Studying was very difficult. One day as I was walking from biology class to my car, and I was talking to myself. I put my hand into the air and said, "Please, God, hold my hand; give me strength." All at once, I came back to where I was: There on the tennis courts I was passing, everyone had stopped playing and was looking at me. I guess they thought, "Boy have these classes been getting to her." But I knew I was not by myself and that God would be with me. God does not call us to ministry and then forsake us. God is there to help us.

Another challenge for women and men alike in responding to a call to a church, to chaplaincy, or other church-related ministries comes when the call means moving. My husband retired one month before we moved to a new church call that was three states away. This meant leaving our home where we had lived for twenty-six years of married life. This was Bob's home as a child, and we had bought it from his parents. Bob gave up his community and friends for me. Responding to God's call of ministry meant sacrifice for all of the family, especially my husband. This move was truly up-rooting—leaving our family, leaving our son at home. Bob was wonderfully supportive of me. We are blessed when we have the support of loved ones.

The biggest challenge for many is dealing with the dynamics of our extended families. They do not always understand our ministry. Parents and in-laws have certain expectations of us. My mother-in-law was Catholic. She respected my call to ministry and even came to my ordination, even though it was totally against her beliefs to come to a Protestant church. (She was from the old school.) Maybe she came because my ordination involved an ecumenical service with some people from the Mennonite community, an Episcopal bishop, and a Catholic nun friend of hers. It was the only time during my ministry that she came to a church where I was serving. During one of my pastorates, the parsonage was across a driveway from the church. My mother-in-law came to visit for ten days, but she would not walk across the driveway to visit my church.

I have also found that people in your home church do not come to hear you preach. Oh, they say, "We are coming to hear you preach someday. Until then we keep up with you through talking to family members and through the newspaper." People who were close friends before I went into the ministry do not come to hear me speak. Maybe I should be more inviting. If all the people who have said they are going to come to church to hear me preach actually *came* to church, the church would be full.

I was the church organist for twenty years in my home church. I believe they do not come because they remember me as who I was and don't think I can do the job even though I have been through college and seminary. It is funny that several times I have been asked to play the organ or piano instead of preaching. It takes time for people to see you in a different way. But it can happen over time and with new experiences. After all, haven't we learned from the life of Jesus? In Matthew 13:54–58, it tells us of Jesus' rejection in his hometown. As Jesus began teaching in the synagogue, the people said, "Where did this man get this wisdom and these deeds of power? Is not this the carpenter's son? Is not his mother called Mary? And are not his brothers James and Joseph and Simon and Judas? And are not all his sisters with us? Where then did this man get all this?" (13:55–56).

In Matthew 10:34–39, Jesus does not promise peace but a sword:

> "Do not think that I have come to bring peace to the earth; I have not come to bring peace, but a sword.
>
> > For I have come to set a man against his father,
> > and a daughter against her mother,
> > and a daughter-in-law against her mother-in-law;
> > and one's foes will be members of one's own
> >   household.
>
> Whoever loves father or mother more than me is not worthy of me, and whoever loves son or daughter more than me is not worthy of me…" (10:34–37)

These are hard sayings. It was not easy for Jesus and it is not easy for us, but if we place God first, "all things are possible with God."

Tresa Quarles, a colleague, says she does not have to balance as much as some of her "sisters do, for I am single. Since I entered seminary at age fifty-five, I studied day and night for three years. It had been a long time since I had been a student; I had been a teacher. It was difficult to have time to visit my siblings, who live in four states. My friends waited for me. My family accepted it with reservation. Even now I know that my plans are subject to change and do not resent that. My vacation plans were postponed recently due to the death of an active church member."[5]

---

[5]Rev. Tresa Quarles, pastor at St. Stephen's United Church of Christ, Harrisonburg, Virginia.

I have planned a vacation that I had to reschedule at the beginning or at the end two times. When I was a pastor in Pennsylvania, I went with a group to Israel and Italy for two weeks. Upon my return, my husband and a church member were there as I got off the plane, waiting to meet me with news that one of our parishioners had died that day. I went straight to the family's home and gave my condolences and spent some quality time with them, listening and praying with them. I was exhausted and hungry, but that could wait. God has a way of giving us the strength we need. He certainly carries us many times. It was some time later that evening that Bob and I had our quality time with dinner in a restaurant. After a good night's sleep I was ready to go again.

One time I went home to Virginia for Christmas Day and returned to Pennsylvania the next day to conduct a funeral. On the way back to Pennsylvania, I ate something that gave me food poisoning. I was so sick. My dear husband went to the drug store and bought me some coke syrup that stopped the vomiting. I was told just to drink that and some ginger ale. Between the two and with the help of God, I made it through the funeral. I didn't know if I was going to have to stop during the service by asking for silent prayer while I ran to the restroom. But, I made it. I was feeling some better, so back to Virginia we went. I was not well and became very ill while trying to eat something else. I ended up in ER in the hospital with three intravenous feedings. That afternoon, we went back to Pennsylvania. That was a vacation to remember. Thank God for understanding family and church members.

When I moved to Virginia, I soon realized that I had to do ministry differently than I had in Pennsylvania, where I had one church—since now I had two. I treated them as one church with many different personalities' and different expectations. We have to realize that we cannot do it all. We need help in balancing family and ministry in the church. Delegation to all is best and helps to develop the gifts of all God's people.

I have tried to recognize the talents and gifts in others, help them recognize their own gifts, and to deepen them in the life of the church. The church is full of people with gifts just waiting to be unleashed. I know sometimes it would be easier for me to do things instead of asking others, but once people begin to take responsibility, they have ownership. It takes time to build relationships and trust, but it is worth it because all benefit from it.

On 9–11, I was on vacation in Arizona visiting with my sister. We were traveling by train, so it took us one week to get home. I was so torn and felt so helpless because I wanted to be with family *and* the church—because they were family. Thank God for cell phones. I called the church moderators for both congregations and asked them each to plan a community prayer service for the coming Sunday evening at the church. These were strong leaders, and I knew they could do it. One church had a service at 5:00 p.m., and the other one had a service at 7:00 p.m. I was in touch with the lay leader who was preaching that Sunday morning. This was an awesome responsibility for him, but he did a beautiful job. These gifted lay leaders held the congregations together, grieved together, and prayed together. I was powerless except through prayer and the cell phone. My family was all right. They worshiped God with their church families and grieved together. Their concern was for Bob and me to make it home. A call to ministry is a call to everyone you are involved with. Some get on board, and some do not. You have to learn what to keep and what to let go. To have balance is to have wisdom and knowledge, and know, "There is a time for everything." When it is not the right time, let it go. Know that God does not call us to ministry and then desert us. God is there to help us through all of our challenges.

Being a minister and a woman brings surprises to many people. In each of the churches I have served, many people stop for help. They need money for gas for their automobile, or a place to spend the night. When the secretary shows them to my office, often they look at me with surprise and say, "Are you the minister? I was not expecting a woman."

In one of the communities where I served as pastor, I was asked by our ministerial association to be in charge of the transient fund. This was a fund that helped homeless people who were traveling through our community. The other churches would send them to our church. I told the consistory (the governing board) at our church what I was going to do. They did not think it was a good idea at first because I was a woman. They felt a man should deal with these situations. However, I did take on that responsibility. The church was supportive. In some situations, I thought they could be right. As time went on, I grew more confident in dealing with many situations and felt blessed in being able to help people. I think women bring sensitivity and kindness to the many situations like these. In several situations, I called on male colleagues to help me out. Once I was called to go to a motel room and talk to a young man who needed counseling. I called a fellow pastor and asked him to go with me. He was more than happy to do so, and it is a blessing we both went. The young man needed our help. I could not have called another woman pastor to help, even if I had wanted to, because I was the only woman minister in our community at that time. However, it was probably best there were a man and a woman there to work with this young man.

Other times, when it comes to counseling, a male pastor has referred women parishioners from other churches in our community to me. I have done the same with a male parishioner by referring him to a male colleague. There has been respect shown in our respective ministries. Of course, a few male colleagues would never ask a woman minister to help out. They probably would not ask a man either.

A woman minister can bring insights into counseling couples that male colleagues may not be able to do. When counseling one couple, I realized what was needed was for the husband to express his love for his wife by showing her attention. They loved one another. They just did not show it. They had been married for thirty years. It had been about ten years since he had taken her out to dinner or sent her flowers. All that was needed was spending quality time with her. By the second counseling session, he had taken her out to dinner and sent her flowers. Women know what another woman needs. A woman needs to feel valued and special. This lady had been giving to her husband for many years.

She needed to feel valued and appreciated. Now, they have a beautiful relationship and enjoy each other's company in traveling and taking time for one another.

Being a minister and a woman is challenging and rewarding. A woman can bring something special to ministry by being who she is. We can be glad that we are women and that God calls us to ministry.

7

The Joys of Ministry

I (Barbara) was so enthusiastic about going into the ministry. I had achieved a lifetime dream. I felt God's call early in my life, but I fought against it. Finally, at the age of forty-two, I could do nothing else but say "yes" to God's calling. I found the greatest peace even though it meant many challenges and a life change for my family and me. I was married and had two children. I went back to college and then on to seminary, taking the equivalent of seven years of courses, going to school all year around, and graduating in five years. An ecclesiastical council from our thirty-six churches in the Shenandoah Association questioned me, and then I was unanimously accepted for ordination.

At that time, I did not know the extent of the joy and blessing ministry would bring. I was going to be able to do all the things I had always enjoyed doing, such as serving God, studying the Bible, and helping people grow in their Christian faith as they faced life's difficult situations. It was exciting to think about the many aspects of ministry that I would be doing. Life would be full and rich.

Wondrously, my dreams and expectations could never compare to the actual joys that I have found in ministry over the last twenty-six years. I will share some of my greatest joys and also the joys of other women in various roles of ministry.

One of the greatest joys of my ministry has been learning from many people of all different ages and backgrounds. Each has blessed my life, and I have learned something from each one. From one lady, I learned about hospitality. We will call her Martha. Every time I went to see her, she had her linen strawberry tablecloth on the dining room table and her best china. The table was spread with cheese and crackers and brownies and the best coffee ever. Martha, her husband George, and I would have a blessing over our feast and then share in the goodies with the most pleasant conversation. Around this table, I learned to know this loving couple and their hopes and dreams for the future. They made me feel important and loved. George and Martha wanted to do something for me, because I was their pastor. It made me feel loved and certainly gave me new strength for the rest of the day. Hospitality is something we can show to others. It lets others know we care about them. I hope I never forget to be hospitable toward others. It doesn't take much to make someone else happy.

Often I ask parishioners if I can visit them at work. Most of the time they are delighted for me to visit. I visited Audrey at her job at the university, where she was a horticulturist. She had developed a coffee plant that could better survive hot weather. She took great pleasure in showing me her plants and what she did for a living. I learned how creative she was in her thinking and how much she cared for other people in trying to help them have a better way of life. This showed me the many kinds of ministry and ways we touch people's lives. I found she also applied her creativity and concern for others in her work in the church. Once, she was the only member who came to church during a blizzard. She arrived by snowmobile, and we had church.

When I first went into the ministry, my husband, Bob, and I left family in the Shenandoah Valley and moved to Happy Valley in Pennsylvania, where we knew no one. Until that time, I had always lived in the same state. We missed our family very much. We had left our daughter and her husband, our son and Bob's mother, plus brothers and sisters. We had left all of our friends. I went to the mailbox every day hoping to get a letter from home, which I usually did.

Soon I had to have a root canal. That meant a new dentist. I shared with him how much I missed everyone back home. As I sat there, not being able to say anything as he worked on my tooth, this Christian man gave me some thoughts of wisdom. He said, "Everywhere you go, you will be blessed with making new friends. Your heart is big enough to hold all of them." This was powerful. My heart has been blessed to overflowing as we have made friends with the most wonderful people in the world.

I have not said anything about those people who have been a challenge to know, but I have learned from them also. I always try to see the positive in people. I found sometimes you have to look harder for it, but you can find it. Sometimes you have to discover what makes people say the things they do and act the way they do. Some instances have been a rude awakening for me.

At the first congregational gathering in one of the churches I began serving, two women waited until everyone had left. They asked, "Do you believe in the Holy Spirit?"

I answered, "Yes."

After this we talked about the power of God's Spirit to lead and direct our lives. During the next year, they would bring more questions to me about faith and belief. Both of these women were Sunday school teachers in the church. I thought they were asking me for information to help them grow in their faith and to help them in their teaching. However, I discovered when I did not say what they wanted to hear, they became upset. I observed in their teaching of their Sunday school class, they put people down if they did not believe the same as these women did. They seemed to have all the right answers. I finally realized I could not trust them. While I thought they were willing learners, they were testing me, checking to see if I would say things they did not believe. They finally said the people in our church and I were going to hell because we were not Christians. Life was really tough for a while. Finally, they both left our congregation and went to another church.

I learned from these women. Some people follow their own agenda to trip up the minister because they have all the answers. Your answers better match theirs, or you are wrong. They find fault with everyone, not only the minister. Some people have to be right all the time. For some, the church is where this all comes out. Unable to control things at work, at school, or at home, they try to control as many things as possible at church. Low self-esteem is at stake in many cases.

Our church survived. The class grew as well, as their faith, with a new teacher who did not put everyone on trial every Sunday. These women found happiness in another church. The joy of ministry is learning to know people, even those who challenge you. All of them teach us many things about life and ministry.

There is the joy of "awe" moments. These are mountaintop experiences that bring joy that you do not forget. One of these mountaintop experiences happened when I was in my first church as a student pastor. Having their first woman pastor—and a student pastor at that—challenged the church. I was the only pastor of the church, and I was only hired part-time. One gentleman was the sweetest man, but he could not see very well, read, or hear. He came to church every Sunday. He and another gentleman always sat on the back row. Since he had these hearing and reading problems, he would try to carry on a conversation during church with this other gentlemen, who sometimes told him in a loud voice to be quiet. What I remember most about this man happened about a month after I started as minister at this church. I was standing in the narthex shaking hands with people as they went out of church. This gentleman came up to me and said, "I have a gift for you. Please open it now." It looked like a box of peanuts, with a picture of them on the side. I was so happy because he had brought me a gift. I opened it, and out jumped this wire cloth snake. Did he laugh when I jumped! So did others! I knew I was accepted at this church. What an "awe" moment.

This same gentleman provided another "awe" moment. When he went to live in a nursing home, I visited him a great deal. Then he had to be admitted to the hospital and became very frightened. My visits helped to calm him. I took him a cross that illuminated in the dark and I placed it on the rail of his bed. I would lean across the rail and hold his hand. When he saw me coming, he would reach his hand up to take mine. We always had a prayer together that brought him peace.

When he died, I went to his viewing. With people all around, I stepped up to the casket. I saw his hand come up to meet mine. It was transparent. I could see through it, but it was his hand. I jumped, startled for a moment. I looked to see if anyone else saw it. Of course, they did not. No one even stirred. I knew it was my gift from God. He was all right now, safe and secure with our heavenly Father. Times like this, when God gives special "awe" moments, bring assurance that I am certainly not in this ministry alone and that someone greater than I is leading and directing my life and ministry. God has called me, and God will not leave me alone to minister. This happening was one of many "awe" moments God gives us as ministers. What a joy a close walk with God brings.

Our own unique ministries bring special joy. Our call to ministry leads us many various places. Every congregation is different and has a major mission. God calls the churches as God calls the pastor, each of us to our own special unique ministry. Tresa Quarles, a United Church of Christ pastor, shares her greatest joy:

> I was a pastor to a declining city church that had had no minister for fourteen months, with guest speakers filling the pulpit on Sunday. There, I discovered people who did not want the church to die, and a great leader, the administrative council president—a woman. We decided on goals and visions and dreams and got to work. In a year we had fifteen new members join us, started children's church, got all the committees active by meeting with them and offering guidance, started a capital fundraising

project, got the youth involved in worship, started a visitation program, and had confirmation classes for seven boys. Attendance jumped from the twenties to the high forties. Excitement fills the church. They want new members, accept diversity, appreciate my work, and love the Lord. We did all of this in spite of a $275,000 arson fire that took us away from our church from December 11, 2004–May 8, 2005.[1]

Becoming a new minister in a church brings its own excitement, with many hopes and dreams for both the pastor and the congregation. Many blessings result when you join in unity to discover what God wants you to do together and then do it. When love is present, the unity and sharing of ministry is blessed.

Bringing healing and change to people's lives creates joy. I went to a church that needed healing after they had endured an unfortunate situation. A disagreement arose over whether the previous pastor should purchase a house or live in the parsonage. This led to a split in the congregation and to the pastor leaving after an eighteen-year pastorate. He became a pastor in a community ten miles away. Many members followed him to the new church. The congregation went through a grieving period. Anger and disappointment changed to forgiveness and acceptance. An interim minister helped them through the process for two years. When I became the pastor, I continued what they had begun. The congregation was ready for a new beginning with new members and programs.

In the first year, I visited all 340 members—both those who remained and those who had left. I listened with compassion and encouraged love and forgiveness. I find the best way to teach and help others is to be a role model. I loved the congregational members. Twenty-four new members were gained the first year I was pastor. We held Bible studies and formed new ministries of mission and evangelism. It took five years for this healing to happen, even though we

---

[1]Rev. Tresa Quarles, pastor at St. Stephen's United Church of Christ, Harrisonburg, Virginia.

moved on from day one with new ministries. It took love and forgiveness to have wholeness.

The healing process began to happen as members shared their feelings. Congregations know it if the pastor truly loves them and loves doing God's ministry. You can see the fruits of your labor in the spiritual journey of the people in the congregation. Seeing healing and change happen is truly a joy and a blessing.

Rev. Geneal Wilson said, "The things I enjoy about ministry are the opportunit[ies] to make a difference. I love to preach. I get excited about that. I get excited about the fact you are invited into people's lives as family. I find that very uplifting and significant. I think about times that are most sacred and precious. I guess I would have to lift up baby dedications, that sort of thing. [Also,] being with people at their bedside in times of crisis is a very sacred space."[2]

One of the greatest joys is hearing others pray. Church members praying out loud doesn't always happen until a trust level is reached and people feel comfortable. Usually the pastor is asked to pray at events and activities.

Early in my ministry at one church, I led a group in a spiritual retreat at a Jesuit Center. I did all the praying out loud when we joined together. A few years later this same group went on another retreat. This time, everyone encircled one member at a time, and we all prayed for that person. How enriching this was for me. My heart overflowed with gratitude to God as I heard people praying from their hearts. My prayers are important, but so are the prayers from all of God's people.

I have a joy of serving others. This is lived out through my call to ministry. I feel I am helping others, and in return I feel blessed. Serving others by providing communion to shut-ins is a blessed and joyous event. One lady who was homebound always had a special place set at her table, with a linen cloth ready for me to place the communion set. I read the Bible, had a few short comments, and prayed. Then we

---

[2]Rev. Geneal Wilson, pastor at Strasburg Christian Church, Strasburg, Virginia.

had communion. She was gracious and expressed gratitude for sharing in this meal together. Sometimes, an elder from the church went with me and did some of the readings. When this dear soul went to the nursing home, she kept providing a special place for us again to have communion. When our church purchased new chairs, her son bought one of the old ones. He refinished it and brought it to the nursing home, where he placed it behind a door. Every time I brought communion, out came that special chair, which became the communion table. It was our center where we received the blessing of this holy meal. It brings joy to my heart to serve the eucharist when means so much to another person. I enjoy providing the eucharist service for people who do not have an opportunity to receive it often. At lease twice a year, the social director of a local nursing home and I work together to have a worship service where all the patients who want communion come together. We do this in the dinning room, since they do not have a chapel. A member of our consistory and I lead a service and share this precious meal together. Since I am also a musician, we sing hymns of faith.

It is heart-warming to place the bread into the feeble hands of a sweet lady or gentleman who cherish that moment. The look of sweet peace and love covers their faces as they receive the bread and the cup. It is nourishment and refreshment for their souls.

I find great joy in serving God. I enjoy being a minister because I love God and I love people. I find in myself that I am a Mary *and* a Martha (Jn. 11). I love to sit at the feet of Jesus and learn like Mary; but I am also like Martha in that I love serving others. It is a joy and blessing to my heart.

I find great satisfaction in doing God's work because I learn to know God even more. I am very thankful for the opportunity to grow in faith. Joy comes from having alone time with God in the quietness of my home, my church, my office, or in the sanctuary of the church, on a spiritual walk, studying, or in a retreat. I have my faith renewed, my hope lifted, and peace and joy rekindled.

I have never liked to exercise physically, but I have found that making my morning walk into a spiritual walk has done several things. It helps me physically, mentally, and spiritually. I read a scripture and ponder it and pray as I walk. At one church I served, I was able stop in the church sanctuary and pray some more before going home. What a blessing and a joy to spend time with God and prepare for the day ahead. The church was my home as well as the parsonage. It is a great joy to have access to God's house at all times.

A joy of ministry involves sacred moments in people's lives. Rev. Debbie Harmon tells about this joy in ministry for her.

> It is being present, and having a "front row seat" at such significant and sacred moments as baptism and weddings. To be the one to plunge [people] into the water of baptism and see their faces as they emerge as a newly baptized member of the family of Christ is amazing. We share that special moment. Each face of someone I have baptized is special. They will always remember me as the one who baptized them. I will always remember sharing in that significant moment in their lives.[3]

A special moment of joy is working with parents as you plan a baptism. Infant *and* believer's baptisms are a part of our tradition in the United Church of Christ. A great joy is working with parents in helping them understand what a wonderful gift they are giving their child. This child will be baptized into the family of God, where there is support from the beginning of their child's faith journey. The Bible says, "A little child shall lead them." This I believe. Many times, I have baptized a child only to have one of the parents who has not been baptized ask for baptism. Often a child's baptism has led to the entire family being baptized.

Moments we share with others are precious. Debbie Harmon says, "I love standing in front of a couple reciting their wedding vows, seeing the tears, or laughter, or both that come with such a moment. To see a bride's face glowing,

---

[3]Rev. Debbie Harmon, pastor at the Edinburg Christian Church, Edinburg, Virginia.

to see the groom stand just a little taller seeing his bride come down the aisle. These are wonderful moments." She remembers an opportunity she had presiding at her cousin's wedding, one of her first weddings to perform. Debbie says, "I remember he looked unusually handsome in his white tux. His bride was so pretty that day, and her cheeks were glowing. We had the service on the front porch of my aunt and uncle's house, and it was a lovely June day. We will always share the moment."

Debbie adds, "In an odd way, funerals are one of the joys of ministry because we have the opportunity to share the gospel, the good news of eternal life, at the most pertinent moment in the life of a family. To walk with a family through such a holy, sacred time is an honor and a joy."

Susie Cameron expresses her precious moments of joy.

> When I think about high moments, of precious moments, what a privilege it is for us to participate in life's most important experiences—deathbeds, funerals, and burials. And, on the other hand, what tremendous elation to stand by as babies are being born. We get that privilege of being with the family at their most private moments, and I count that a real privilege to be included as a part of the family. I find because of that I've made a lot of friends. I know a lot about the families of my church members that the church members don't know about each other. I think that's a real privilege of our calling. It's fun to watch the families because it's a bittersweet moment. They have family time together that they usually don't get, and usually they're having a good time together. I like that.

When death draws near, sometimes prayer or a song of faith brings comfort to another. Others feel the love of God surrounding them through all of us as ministers who are willing to experience this transition with them. It is a difficult time, but one of joy when you know you have helped another person find his or her way into eternity with God.

I was called to the hospital for a church member's friend who was dying. I was not sure where this man was in his faith journey or how his heart was with Christ. As I introduced myself and sat by his side, he started to tell me his life story—about his family, his faith, and his lack of commitment to Christ. He talked about how he had pulled away from Christ. We then talked about Christ's love, mercy, and forgiveness. I know he felt loved. I gave him a small wooden cross, which he held tightly in his hand. When he died several days later, the cross was still in his hand. He died in peace and hope of a glorious future.

A joy in ministry is being creative with ministry by using our gifts. Ann Graves is an intentional interim minister. She says her greatest joy in ministry

> …is being able to bring all of my gifts together in a way that serves God and makes a difference to others. Although I did not set out to do interim ministry, it is well suited to my personality. It has been a good place for me most of the time, and I think has given me an opportunity to seriously impact most of the churches I have served. What I have come to appreciate is that these are by nature shorter-term ministries, though the longest one was three years. The greatest joy is helping a congregation move from a place of despair, bewilderment, often devastation, to a place of hope and renewed energy as they anticipate the arrival of a new pastor.[4]

Serving in my churches, I have tried to stick to my ministry of preaching, pastoral care, and administration in using my gifts, even though I was a church organist for twenty years before becoming an ordained pastoral minister. I have let the musicians in the church use their gifts (and my gift of music only when needed). However, it has been a joy when my gift of music is needed. At one of my churches, we had a contemporary service once a month. It was in this service that I planned the music and selected the contemporary music to

---

[4]Rev. Ann Graves, interim pastor, State College, Pennsylvania.

play in the CD player. One Sunday, after the first hymn was sung, the CD player would not work. It was time for the choir anthem. The choir took their places in front of the church and waited while I pushed this button and that button on the player, but nothing happened. It would not play. I said to myself softly, "Just have patience; take your time." About that time, I heard one of the choir members say, "My patience is wearing out." I knew something else needed to happen. There must be another way. I picked up the sheet music, circled around the choir to the piano, and said, "I will play for you." Afterward, I was praying, "Thank-you God for the gift to play the piano, and that we made it through." I knew I could not give the sheet music to the pianist, who had never seen that piece of music; therefore, I had to do the next best thing. Actually, everyone after church said, "I would rather hear you play than that CD player." By the next time we had the contemporary service, I had a new, uncomplicated player. Before the choir processed, we had an additional prayer for the CD player and me—but mainly for me. It worked perfectly. Faith was restored in the electronic world.

Another joy of using our gifts in ministry is to work as a team. We cannot do everything by ourselves. I could not have survived serving two churches at one time without the work of team ministry. I speak of survival meaning the churches having active vital ministries and serving the community in mission. The church is made up of many gifted people who are willing to use their gifts and talents if asked. It is a joy to plan together as members use their gifts to the honor and glory of God. It is fun and a joy to see the creativity come alive in a group as people share ideas. Members of the group must be open not only to think creatively and use their gifts but they must be open to other people and their ideas. It is only as we give our power away that we will become powerful. When we can work together, we empower one another. As we work together, more is accomplished. In teamwork, respect and openness to listen to other people's ideas is present. Teamwork takes love, knowing that we are all children of God created differently and gifted for ministry. As we look at one another, we can see Christ in each other. We can use our ideas and creative thinking, but we can also listen and grow from others. Encouragement to others helps them develop their gifts. This has been one of the greatest joys of my ministry in every church that I have served: working in unity in spite of diversity.

At one of the churches I served, we had a worship and music ministry in which a team of twelve people planned worship for months ahead. Beautiful services came out of these meetings. Fun and laughter was included as we planned skits, clown ministry, music from different cultures, and much more.

At this same church, a junior youth choir met every Wednesday following school from September through May. It was run by a team of six people. One gentleman came into the church and made popcorn, and put it and cookies on each chair so the children would have a snack when getting off the school bus. Someone would meet the bus. Someone planned an opening worship service, and the main choir director led the music. It was planned down to every detail. Once a month, the children planned the music for worship and sang an anthem. They also had a bell choir. The children grew in appreciation of the love of God and the care of people who helped them blossom into beautiful young Christians. They were happy and it showed on their faces. It is a joy to see so many people ministering together using their gifts—from making popcorn, to directing music, and everything between.

Preparing and delivering sermons are part of the joy of being creative and using the gifts God has given to us for ministry. Susie Cameron said, "The whole process of preparing, study, and the delivery makes Sunday a high moment of joy in ministry. I love the whole process. I love the creative part of it."

Geneal Wilson adds,

I think one of the things that I find with preaching that keeps me really excited about it is, it's like every week I have an opportunity and I reach a place where I think, "Yes, this is really true." It affirms my faith as I delve into the scripture again and draw those parallels between what's going on there and what I've experienced that says, "Yes, this is real and this is true." It calls for creativity, although I will say I do need quiet time and away time. If I don't have that, my preaching is not good. I just have to have some unstructured time, wandering around.

A joy in ministry is working ecumenically with my colleagues. I am very ecumenical. I grew up Baptist, married into the United Church of Christ, went to a Mennonite Seminary, and worked on doctoral degree at a Presbyterian Seminary. I have had the privilege of conducting several weddings with priests and one with a rabbi. Of course, in the Roman Catholic Church, I was only allowed to read scripture, but I was there. The rabbi and I conducted a wedding in a neutral pulpit at a Unitarian church. The rabbi read the blessings in Hebrew, and I read then in English. I preached the sermon, and someone sang the Lord's Prayer. The rabbi led the service of breaking the glass.

Most of all, I have enjoyed working on community services and missions with clergy from all denominations— some mainline and some non-mainline. Debbie Harmon said, "Whether comparing notes on what to preach on Sunday, to comparing notes (complaining!) about other aspects of ministry, try to stay connected to a circle of other ministers. I participate in [a] weekly lectionary group, a monthly meeting of ministers in my town, a monthly meeting of ministers in my denominational district, and a clergy singing group. The support and encouragement is a great reinforcement to my ministry."

Working with your ecumenical brothers and sister is a joy and often just plain fun. When I was serving a United Church of Christ in Centre Hall, Pennsylvania, our small town had only two other churches—Lutheran and United Methodist. One year, April's Fools Day came on Sunday. Our three churches had a wonderful working relationship, so the other two pastors and I decided we would exchange pulpits without letting out congregations know ahead of time. Our congregational members were really surprised. At first they could not understand why another pastor was at their church. It was fun and accepted.

That day, I went to the Lutheran church. When I got up to preach, I said, "Would you believe that I am your minister with a new hairdo?" You see, their minister was a he with not as much hair as I had. The next Sunday, he continued the drama by wearing a wig that looked just like my hair and said, "Well, I though I would come back again this Sunday."

We ministers had a great deal of fun and laughter, but, even more important, a great respect and support of one another and the ministries we shared. Even though I live in another community many miles away from these ministers, I always know that they are there to support me. They have been added to the many other people who I carry in my heart. You see, our hearts are big enough to keep letting others in. They are our present-day "cloud of witnesses."

Joys are shared with members of our congregations. We all have stories to remember that make our hearts leap with joy. Tresa Quarles tells about an experience with an older parishioner. She was taking her to a doctor's appointment. Tresa says, "She asked me to drive through the cemetery, which was close by, for she had little interest in living or anything else. She said she knew she would not be coming back home, but would be going there instead. As we admired the flowers that had been placed there for Easter, she forgot what we were doing there.

After the doctor's appointment (anxiety syndrome), we passed a frozen custard stand. I suggested we partake of some good custard. She had a double dip of raspberry, and I had vanilla. Then we laughed all the way home."

Laughter sounded often in the choir at a little country church I served. They had a wonderful sense of humor and teased me a great deal. Some of the men in the choir chewed tobacco—except on Sunday mornings when they sang in the choir. They asked me if they could place a spittoon next to the choir so they could chew during church. They said they could sing better if they could chew. Naturally, they did not get the spittoon. But we laughed about it.

Sometimes we forget how precious our church members are. When we can get to know them, we can have greater relationships and ministry.

A joy in ministry is acceptance and support from your congregation. Each church I have served had an initial concern about having a woman minister. They were not sure they were ready for this. Acceptance grew gradually. With it came wonderful support for me and our ministry together. As a student, I served a small church as part-time student pastor, the only staff member. We agreed I would work twenty hours a week. What a joy when everyone from the church came to graduation at the seminary! They held a reception at church afterward. At this church my ecclesiastical council and my ordination took place. I was their first woman pastor and student pastor. Following my time there, there have been several others student pastors. This has become the church's mission: to help students as they go through seminary. I know that, for me, it helped wondrously with my student loan and also gave me on-the-job training. They helped make my seminary education a joy. When I was studying the gospel of John in seminary, I taught a Bible study on it at church. When I was getting ready to conduct my first funeral, I went to class at the seminary before the time of the funeral. My teacher and the class prayed with me. What a blessing to have support not only of the church but also of my professors and fellow students. The two pastors who followed me at the church were women. I found joy in knowing the church accepted and supported me as a woman and as a student.

My first fulltime pastorate was in Pennsylvania. They accepted me as a woman pastor and a pastor from the South. At first, being from the South was more of an issue than my being a woman. They always laughed when I read the passage of scripture about "Moses and the burning bush." When you are from the South and you say "bush," it sounds very different than when someone from the North pronounces it. One thing I learned—when this lady from the South got into their hearts, they accepted me. We had a wonderful, loving relationship. When I had some family celebrations back in Virginia, a large group of church people attended. Today, we receive visits from many of our friends from the North.

My third pastorate was with two churches. In my third year as pastor of these churches, I had to have surgery and be off work for six weeks. The church people were wonderful caregivers, understanding and compassionate. I planned all of the services before I left, but they carried them out. We had excellent speakers within both churches. One of the young men preached on Father's Day. The congregation applauded him and his message. I heard the tape of the service. He was good. I teased him about this. He received applause, and I never did. So, one Sunday, the congregation applauded me. I think they just did this because they felt I needed encouragement. Whatever the reason, I accepted it graciously. I was so proud of the way both churches handled my illness. During this six-week period of time, two members of one of the churches died. I was so sorry I could not attend the funerals, but I called family members and had prayer on the phone with them.

The first Sunday back from my surgery, some of the men had moved the pulpit down from the chancel area to the same level as the congregation so I would not have to walk up the steps. How thoughtful they were.

Following the surgery, I had to be careful what I ate. Everyone knew I could not eat anything with nuts in it, so at dinners they always made sure to make something for me that did not have nuts.

What a joy it is to have congregations that minister to the pastor when needed. We are there for one another. These are congregations empowered to do ministry using their gifts. They are caring and compassionate, not only to the pastor, but also to other members in the congregations and in the community. When the church is living out the "good news of Jesus Christ," it is a joy.

A joy in ministry is teaching others. My last confirmation class was five girls who were creative and energetic. On confirmation Sunday, they assisted in conducting the worship service. For the prelude and prayer response, one played the flute and another played the clarinet. Three sang "Amazing

Grace" while the other two other girls did a liturgical dance. It was beautiful.

While in confirmation class, we covered many subjects, from church history to the death and resurrection of Jesus. We studied the Old and New Testament stories. On the last day of class, I gave them an exam. One of the questions was, "What did you learn in confirmation class?" Everyone answered in one form or another, "to love God and to love people; do unto others as you would have them do unto you." Yes, they learned church history and all of the other stories, but they also got what the Christian faith is all about.

Last, but not least, it is joy of having it all: my family (husband and children), my church family, and my friends all over the community who have blessed my life. My husband and I were able to travel to many places that we would never have been able to if I had not been a pastor. Many opportunities were made available to us as we added vacation time to trips to the conference and General Synod of the United Church of Christ.

Whether or not we have a spouse and children, we all have the church family of which we are a part. They can be a blessing to us. If we find ourselves in a church that is not, hopefully, we can find a church that is a blessing.

Being called by God to the ministry is a joy in itself. Serving God through the call brings blessings to our lives and the congregations we serve.

8

Keep on, Sisters!

I (Barbara) have been in the pastoral ministry for twenty-two years. I knew when I was a little girl of ten years old, playing church, that I wanted to be a minister. I felt this tugging at my heart all of my life to go into ministry, but I resisted until I could not resist it anymore. At the age of forty-two, I responded to God's calling. It was then that I found the greatest peace in my heart and in my life.

For a long time, I thought of every reason I could for not following what I knew I was meant to do. I was doing ministry in my own way, helping everyone I could. I thought this was enough. I made lots of excuses. I decided I lived too far from college, which was about eighteen miles from home. After all, I could not drive in the snow in winter. I was too old. I did not have the funds. My husband would never approve. However, it didn't matter how many excuses I made to myself, there was something missing. It was through the encouragement of friends and my association conference minister, Rev. Dr. Bernie Zerkel, that I decided to step out in faith. This meant going back to college and seminary. It was through this experience that my gifts of ministry were affirmed. It was through the affirmation and encouragement of my family, friends, and classmates that I was able to pursue this career.

We encourage any women reading this and considering ministry, or just going into ministry, to follow your calling. It is fulfilling to know that God has called you and you have responded. It is not always easy, but it is rewarding as you make a difference in other people's lives.

Geneal Wilson's words of encouragement are, "I would encourage women to enter ministry, but I would say to do it only because you feel a call that cannot be denied. You are not going to find your self-esteem boosted. You are not going to find support where you expect to find support. My advice would be to live authentically."[1]

Pastoral ministry in a church is not the only ministry option we have. There are many areas of ministry. For example, some areas of ministry are: chaplaincy, interim, interfaith, pastoral in a church setting, and others. We encourage you to explore these. Whatever your call, it will be a blessing to you. Judy Blonski, an ordained interfaith minister, was visiting recently at the church I serve in Virginia. We met several years ago when she was visiting some of her relatives who were members of this church. I asked her to lead a prayer in our service. Following the prayer, we sang the hymn, "Here I Am, Lord." After the service she shared these words with me:

> After praying, I rejoined my husband in the pew. I broke down and wept as the congregation began singing the final old familiar hymn, "Here I Am, Lord." The tears flowed from a deep well within my being. There were so many emotions swirling within my heart. Yes, it is sometimes lonely traveling around, serving where I am needed and, yes, it would be so much simpler to settle down in one spot and minister as a pastor... But I realized I do have a flock, my congregation. It's everywhere. The gut-level sobbing was gratitude for the joy and the satisfaction I have

---

[1]Rev. Geneal Wilson, pastor at Strasburg Christian Church, Strasburg, Virginia.

had and will continue to receive, for my prayers are constantly being answered. "Here I Am, Lord. Use my life to your glory." Amen, Peace, Amen.[2]

Women have many gifts and abilities to give to ministry. Ann Graves' words to a women going into the ministry are:

I would tell her to go for it! There is a huge need for good ministers, and I believe women have many gifts for ministry. These days, many strides have been made, though there are still many more to go. I believe women have the ability to transform the way churches function. Because of a woman's generally more collegial style of working, many congregations can benefit from being encouraged to engage more fully in ministry themselves. Women have the ability to teach churches that they can do many things for themselves, so that the pastor can be the teacher, spiritual leader, and interpreter.

Balancing the role of pastor with that of family needs and responsibility is difficult, but it has always been that way for women, no matter what choices they make. However, if a woman is married, then there needs to be total support from her partner. Family relationships in the church have always been challenging, no matter which partner is the pastor! Developing support outside the church is really important.[3]

Ann gives good advice about developing support systems outside the church. Women are gifted for ministry, but we need the support and encouragement of others. I had a New Testament professor in college who knew that the students who were going into pastoral ministry would need a support system. He gave some of his students their first experience of one.

[2]Rev. Judy Blonski, All Faiths Dialogue and Celebration, San Marcos, California.

[3]Rev. Ann Graves, interim pastor, State College, Pennsylvania.

He invited a small group of three of us to have lunch with him. He came for a few moments and said, "I thought it would be good for you to learn to know one another since the three of you are going to seminary and into ministry." Then he left. He provided us with our first support group. I found throughout my ministry that I need such a group. I encourage you to have a support group who will be there to help you discern what God is calling you to do. They are there to affirm your giftedness and calling.

Tresa Quarles finds support outside the church in another way. She shares, "I have a dear friend outside the church who lives in a nearby town. We have had breakfast on Saturdays for fifteen to twenty years. She reads my sermons and listens to me."[4]

This helps to nurture Tresa as well as her friend. It is a good support system for both. What you give away comes back to you.

We encourage women to go into ministry. We encourage you not only to have a support system but also to take care of your physical, emotional, and spiritual self in other ways. Jesus had to draw away from the crowds and from his disciples to go into the mountains to pray. We can learn from his example.

I would advise you to take retreats often. Some of my friends go for a week to a retreat area. Others go for longer periods of time. Retreats are a way of getting away from the everyday routine. We need time to refresh our souls and minds. When I was serving a church in a town where there were only two other churches, the pastors and I went on a one-day retreat once a month. We went away from our church settings to a park, a retreat area, or to another church. Here we spent some time in silent meditation and prayer during the morning and then gathered back together and ate our bag lunches. We shared a time of fellowship. Then we had some more silence followed by a time to share some of the

---

[4]Rev. Tresa Quarles, pastor at St. Stephens United Church of Christ, Harrisonburg, Virginia.

learnings from our time alone with God. It was a blessed time of renewal and support of one another's ministry.

At one time in my ministry, I knew I needed something more. I felt I was spiritually drying up. I heard about a program for training for spiritual directors. I decided to take this two-year course. This gave me another day a month away for mediation and leaning. During the year, there were two different two-day retreats. They involved a lot of traveling because we met about two hours from where I lived. I met two other ladies from a nearby town who traveled with me. The trip to and from the training program became a time for sharing the many things going on in our lives. We became a wonderful support group for one another. We became prayer partners. Today, we still keep in touch even though this training took place eleven years ago.

This training gave new life to my spiritual life. I felt renewed and refreshed. I became a better pastor because of this. It has led me to teach workshops on contemplative prayer. It also helped to bring direction to my life and led me into new avenues of ministry. From here, I began a doctorial degree program in spirituality. I led retreats for women at the Jesuit Center.

As a part of our training in spiritual direction, a requirement was to go on our own private retreat. This I did by going to a private retreat center for two days one October. I stayed in an old house that was a part of this center. The man who was the director of the center checked on me once to make sure everything was all right, and otherwise it was a private retreat. We need time alone to spend with God. I took holy communion and sat at a picnic table out under a tree. There I had communion with Christ, of whom I was a guest at his table.

I enjoyed this private time with God, but I was glad to get back to my family and the church. I was ready to do ministry in a freshness of heart and mind. Two days were enough for me, but I knew a lady in my class that went on a thirty-day retreat. Whatever time you can allow for a retreat is an opportunity to learn to know yourself better and to have solitude with God. We need a balance between solitude and community and between quietness and conversation. The scripture tells us, "Be still, and know that I am God" (Ps. 46:10a).

A spiritual director or mentor is of great importance to walk with us in our spiritual journey. As Jesus walked with the disciples on the road to Emmaus, so Jesus walks with us. But he also shows how helpful it is to have someone walk alongside you on your journey, asking the questions that lead you to a deeper level of faith. I have had three spiritual directors. Each one was very different in his or her approach to our time together. We met once a month for an hour, in which we explored God's leading for me in my life. One of the directors started with prayer, asking us where God would lead us that day. Actually, he liked to have the questions beforehand so he would have time to think about them and to pray about where our time together might go. We carried on more of a conversation. I knew this spiritual guide many years, and he still helps me when I need some answers to some issue. He is always available even though technically he is not my spiritual guide. He had to discontinue being a spiritual guide for people in the area where we live because of health reasons and the distance he had to travel. He knows me better than anyone else besides my family.

I had another spiritual guide who prayed with me and led me through some spiritual meditations. With another person providing the opportunity, God can speak to us in wondrous ways. This guide was very spiritual in a different way from the first one. The first one was very structured, but not this one. With the first one, we usually knew where we wanted to go, and we had some solutions at the end. With the second one, I was only beginning to find the solutions when I left the session.

The third spiritual leader I had was a woman. She was very soft spoken and gentle. We always began with my lighting a candle, and ended by putting it out. After lighting the candle, we had a prayer to ask where God would have us go. In these sessions there was a great deal of silence, during which I spent time in mediation and prayer. Then I shared what God had showed me. Some prayer exercises brought me great insight, comfort, and direction. I always came away feeling much better and knowing this was between God and me.

It is important to be on a regular monthly schedule with a spiritual guide, because your spiritual life suffers if you do not take care of your soul. You certainly also gain great help by doing prayer exercises and meditation alone. We need to do this as well as having a spiritual guide to share our insights with. I have always found that, with the spiritual guide, God has given him or her insights into our discussion. The guide would share them with me and ask questions that helped me to see other things. He or she would share scriptures and resources that were very helpful.

I recommend everyone have a spiritual guide, especially if you are in the ministry. A minister has the opportunity to mentor parishioners. When you are close to the heart of God, you can help others gain that same closeness. I have even done some spiritual exercises in worship and have written some exercises in the church newsletter for people to do at home. Staying close to the heart of God helps us to know how God is working in our lives and how to have a vital ministry. This is another way of showing our parishioners that we care about them.

As women in the ministry, we need time to worship. Even though I feel I am worshiping as I lead worship, it is good to have time to worship when you are not leading it. A local church has a monthly Sunday evening Taizé service. Every chance I have, I go to this service. I have a colleague who is the pastor of another denomination and whose service is at 11:00 a.m. on Sundays. She goes to another denomination for worship at 8:30 a.m. These are ways that we can praise God in worship without our having to lead.

It is very important that a pastor take care of herself. Tresa Quarles reserves days to nurture her soul. On these days she refuses to be everyone's pastor. "I decline requests to go to the hospital to see everyone's aunt, uncle, grandmother, or grandfather."

In being true to others, you need to remain true to yourself and to take care of yourself physically and emotionally as well as spiritually.

Tresa Quarles says, "Take some down time. Watch the World Series or 'The Price Is Right.'" She offers some other possibilities: "I write stories; I go to the wellness center and work out; I have a dog and a daily walking routine, all seasons."

Ann Graves says:

> I try to be faithful in taking my day off each week. On that day, I really endeavor to not do anything that is related to my church work. I love to sew, and find that putting my creative spirit to work on a sewing project is restorative for me. It engages all of my efforts in a very different way. I also make it a point to take at least a month or two, if possible, between my interim assignments. I find that interim ministry is very intense and that a month or two off really makes a difference when I start a new ministry. Fortunately, I am blessed with a husband whose work supports us well, so that I can afford to do this.

I have a daughter who is a nutritionist and who weighs ninety-four pounds at forty-six years old. She helps me a lot with my eating the right foods; however, with my busy schedule, I do not always eat as I know I should. For women in the ministry, it is difficult to find time to cook proper nutritional meals. Fast food is simpler. Not taking time to eat properly can lead to serious health problems. To be able to care for others in our congregations, we must take care of ourselves.

Laughter is good for the soul and our whole being. Laughing with others and having a positive attitude makes everything look different. Even laughter during the sermon makes everyone feel better. Many times I start my sermon with a funny story, or I include one somewhere within the sermon. I use basically the same sermon each week for the two churches I serve. One church will laugh at my stories, and the other one does not always. I have to be very careful with my stories. Sometimes I use them only at one church. These are stories with a sermon in them as well as them being in the sermon.

Tresa Quarles advises women going into ministry or those who are already in the ministry:

> Remember the first anniversary of a death for widows and widowers. Take some food to the family that has had a death…The oldest woman there in the church will say, "I've been to a lot of funerals, but I've never known the minister to bring something." You'll be proud that you're a woman in the ministry. Work alongside your parishioners no matter what they are doing: unpacking after a fire, doing yard work, having a rummage sale, etc. But, also remember other special days such as wedding anniversaries and birthdays. A call, visit, or card is wonderful to show a parishioner that you have remembered them and they are special.

A woman in the ministry helps to make life better for herself and others. We need to include everyone in all phases of the church life—young and old. Rev. Quarles advises, "Include the children and youth in all your programs. Likewise, involve the older members. They may say to you, 'No one ever asked me to do anything, once I got old.' All are valuable."

One time, I invited this lady in the church to go with me to an Easter pageant at another church. This was the beginning of new life for her. She had been inactive in the congregation, but, after this, she blossomed into an active church member taking part in leading events and serving as an elder in the church. All that is necessary sometimes for people to realize someone cares about them is to show kindness to them, and to show that they are valuable.

Know your congregations—what will work and what will not. Every congregation is different. It takes awhile for you to know everything about them and what works, and how. But don't give up! You never take anything away from people; you just add to it. I have found it takes time for congregations and ministers to learn to trust one another. Some ministers give up too soon and move on. When a minister does this and does not deal with the problems, they go with the minister to the next place. Susie Cameron advises, "Go for the long haul. There's probably no 'easy' church so go in with the idea you'll see things accomplished."[5]

It has not always been easy for me in my ministries. At one church, I knew there were people against me because I was a woman minister. They told me themselves. Some left the church when they knew I had been accepted to be the new minister. Others stayed a year and then left. Others learned to accept me and stayed. Building relationships takes time and the desire of both parties. My advice to women in the ministry is to be brave and courageous. It helps in caring and living.

A gentleman in one of my churches gave me and everyone else a difficult time. At one consistory meeting, he was very mean and disrespectful. I was ready to cry. Instead of giving up and doing what I wanted to do, I looked at him and said with all of my heart, "Don't you know I love you and the members of this church?" We had a great relationship after that. He knew I loved him as his pastor, and so did the congregation.

My husband has always been my best minister. My husband tells me to be kind to people even when they are mean to me. He is a great minister with very good advice. A little kindness goes a long way. Sometimes the only Christ people see is the Christ in us.

Tresa Quarles gives good advice for ministering:

> Remember there is always [at least] one disgruntled man or woman in all churches, who take notes during the sermon and says, as you shake hands, "Just a few helpful hints for you." Thank each one and put the note[s] in your pocket. Likewise, there will be one spinster who tells you how to handle the children. Thank her, too.

---

[5]Rev. Susie Cameron, pastor at East Lynn Christian Church, Anderson, Indiana.

Don't let your job description require that you stock the bathroom with toilet paper, put Clorox in the commode. Or turn the air conditioning and heat on."

Ministry is a challenge, but most of all it is a calling. It is one that is fulfilling. Rev. Quarles also advises, "Look for the rainbows." These rainbows are positive moments in our ministry. They are the light at the end of the tunnel. They are promises to us that God is with us and things are working out. Wonderful stories from people in ministry show witness to these rainbows.

Ann Graves recalls:

One of the special moments for me occurred when I was the interim pastor of a church in an academic community with many foreign students. A family from South Korea started attending the church—Mom and Dad and young son. The mother could barely speak English, though her husband was in an advanced graduate study program. They started attending the church as a way to find community support and learn more about Americans. As time went on, the congregation befriended them. Eventually a daughter was born. They became involved in a Korean church group, and the mother attended Bible study with the group, along with faithful worship attendance each week. About six months after the baby was born, the mother asked for me to visit with them. During the visit she said that she had become Christian and wanted to be baptized along with her baby daughter. We spent a long time talking about how this might separate her from her family, who were all Buddhist. Eventually, the whole family asked to be baptized and become members of the church. It was a very holy moment for me to do this. Adding to this was the family [who] sponsored them. They were longtime members of the church who had adopted an international family of children, one of whom was also South Korean! What a joy that day was.

Ann Graves continues:

Another memorable moment came in a wedding. The bride came from a Roman Catholic family. The bride's sister and her family were very active in their Catholic church. At the wedding reception, the sister told me that her ten-year-old daughter turned to her during the ceremony and whispered that someday she hoped she could be a priest, just like "her," pointing at me! I replied that I hoped by the time she grew up that perhaps that would be possible! However, the way things are going, I suspect not.

Tresa Quarles recalls:

While I was completing a teaching career before going to seminary, I was a lay speaker for the United Methodists. Each Sunday I would go to two little churches to lead the worship service, while the regular pastor went to the other two churches on the charge. There was no bulletin, sometimes a piano player who struck some of the right keys, but always a big welcome. At one of the little churches the choir loft was full, so just before I preached I called on them to sing. To my surprise, they were not the choir. They got to sit there every Sunday, because their grandfather had built the church... Amazing grace!

Sometimes our rainbows are experiences that happen to us that make us laugh and appreciate that in ministry we are not always doing the same thing in the same ways.

We have all kinds of experiences we will never forget. Rev. Quarles tells a funny story:

Several years ago while I was conducting a funeral at a local funeral home, the funeral director instructed me to look at him and nod when my part of the service was over. Throughout most of the service, he stood at the back of the chapel like a sentry, but near the end of the funeral the doorbell rang. He disappeared. I completed my part, so I sat down.

After what seemed to be a long time, he still had not returned, so I looked over at the organist with an exasperated look and nodded my head. To my great relief, she started playing. After she had played eight or ten hymns, the funeral director came back to his post, and I stood and nodded to him… "And the band played on…and on."

I will never forget a dear little lady in one of my congregations who invited me to attend a play with her that was being presented at our local university. She said she would drive. She picked me up in her big car—and it *was* big. I do not know the makes of cars, so I do not know what kind it was, but I know it was large. We drove to the university. When we were about two blocks from it on a deserted street, I noticed we were driving on the bike route. Here we were on the sidewalk that was supposed to be used mostly by cyclists. I said very timidly, "I think somehow we are driving on the sidewalk." She looked up over the steering wheel (since she was so tiny, she was lower than the steering wheel), and said so calmly, "Well, dear, I believe we are. Oh, well, we will just keep going to the end of the sidewalk. Then we will come off of it." I was praying that we would not meet a bicyclist or a pedestrian on that sidewalk. When we got to the end, down we went with a big bump. But we made it. I believe no one even saw us, since there were no cars on this street either. We made it safely to the play, enjoyed it immensely, and then returned home safely.

I have so much fun as a pastor because I am able to meet so many interesting people. There were so many rainbows. I learned something from everyone I met. I have had many funerals in my years of ministry, and not one of them has been alike. Each person who died was a unique individual. As I prepared for my sermons, I made a list of everything I knew about each one, and always a theme would emerge. The theme was always different for each person. God made us each special. The psalmist knew it, "For it was you who formed my inward parts; / you knit me together in my mother's womb. / I praise you, for I am fearfully and wonderfully made. / Wonderful are your works; / that I know very well" (Ps. 139:13–14). There is always more to people than meets the eye. We just need to get to know them. Each person has something to offer to us as we share the gospel of Christ with him or her.

For women going into ministry or women in the ministry already, know you make a difference in other people's lives. You bring about change. You help to bring joy, hope, love, comfort, and peace to others. We each cherish many insightful and sacred moments when we have been able to be there for someone.

Tresa Quarles relates:

> One of my most sacred moments was during my first interim. That night an old railroad man's family, his physician (who lived next door), and I waited for his death. His physician had called me and invited me to be with him and the family, because he didn't think that he would live through the night. We sat around and drank coffee, and waited...and waited... Midnight came...2:00 a.m. came. Just before the sun came up, a cardinal came and sat in a tree and sang its heart out...and the cardinal stopped...and Elwood's heart stopped. "He had made his last run."

Every year for seven years, I conducted a Christmas Eve service for patients at the nearby psychiatric hospital. Usually the number of teenagers there was very high. So much desperation—but even more hope—filled the room where we worshiped. These services were some of the most rewarding services I have conducted, because they brought love and hope to these precious people. The story of Jesus' birth is one that never changes, but in a way is new every year because it brings new life for all. It fills us with a confidence that God loves us and cares for us because God gave us Jesus, God's own Son. It is new and fresh for those who hear it and those who tell it.

The first time I held worship at the psychiatric hospital, I was apprehensive. I prayed that God would be before me working things out in the hearts of others. After praying, I knew with assurance God would. Our God is a "go ahead" God. Deborah reminded Barak as they went to battle, "The LORD is indeed going out before you" (Judg. 4:14). God goes with us everywhere. When Joshua took over for Moses to lead the children of Israel into the promised land, God told Joshua, "I hereby command you: Be strong and courageous; do not be frightened or dismayed, for the LORD your God is with you wherever you go" (Josh. 1:9). God is with us; we need not be afraid.

As a pastor, I have seen God's grace and mercy in lives. This is what we preach, and this is what we experience in our lives and in the lives of others. We are God's children who are called to share our faith and to help provide the means to receive God's healing, grace, and mercy. I have been touched by God's grace and love as I have seen the eyes of faith look up during a prayer and a blessing during healing services. I have witnessed as God transforms the lives of others: a marriage in which the couple are trying to make it a marriage again, and God's grace in the lives of others when the best thing has been for them to divorce.

God's grace came to a young woman who had cancer. As the elders and I held an anointing service in her home, her pain left her, and her swelling went down. She was not cured of cancer, but she was filled with grace and mercy for the pain to let up. When she went to the hospital for the last time before she died, she witnessed to others around her about Christ. God's grace was there for eternal life, where there is no more pain and suffering.

I saw another man who had had a terrible stroke. Even survival was questioned, but by the grace and mercy of God, he is leading a vital life—different than life before the stroke, but very full and meaningful.

Ministry for women is rewarding and meaningful. We have something special to give to others. Many times one of my male colleagues will send a woman parishioner of theirs to me for counseling. It is easier for them to talk to a woman. I am glad that I can be there for them.

I know God has called me to ministry. Even though I am retiring soon, I know that I will always be a minister. God is calling me to another kind of ministry. God will send people my way to minister to. I hope and pray I have the grace and the insight to recognize these people as God sends them. May you too, recognize God's calling of you to ministry and walk with God to change others' lives forever and, in the process, your own.

God loves you. God will take care of you.
Expect people to like a woman minister![6]

---

[6]Rev. Quarles.